HOW TO INVEST RETIREMENT ACCOUNTS IN REAL ESTATE

Make your money work for you twice as hard

Edward Tamayo

Aurora Press
How to Invest Retirement Accounts In Real Estate

ISBN: 978-0-9797623-5-2

Notice of Rights

Notice of Liability
The information given in this book is written in good faith. Even though the content of this book has been researched, some portions could be considered speculative in their own nature. Therefore, the information should be used responsibly and at your own discretion. The information in this book is distributed on an "as is" basis, without warranty. Neither the author, the publisher, nor the companies owned by the author shall have any liability to any person or entity with respect to any loss or damage caused by or alleged to be caused directly or indirectly by the information contained in this book.

This publication is designed to provide accurate and authoritative information regarding the subject matter covered. It is sold with the understanding that the publisher is not engaged in providing financial or legal advice.

This book is
dedicated to my parents,
who opened a big door
to the world for me

Table of Contents

Introduction

- Robert Kiyosaki, author

The investment decisions you make today, including the decision not to invest, will determine the kind of life you will be able to enjoy once that regular income stops rolling in.

While there are multiple ways to invest for retirement and build your wealth, we have seen time and time again that real estate investing is a clear winner. In this book, we talk about doing so with your current 401(k) or individual retirement account (IRA).

No matter what stage of retirement planning you're in, this book will give you options to diversify from traditional stocks and mutual funds, as well as provide better alternatives to increase your net worth and retire with more money.

Drawing on my own path to financial independence, this book will introduce you to the cornerstones of wealth-building real estate, while at the same time minimizing taxes. Through this approach, you will not only make more money, but ultimately get to keep more of what you make.

Who should read this book?

Anyone who wants to increase their income and increase their net worth with passive investments. If you have a job and want to make sure you put those hard-earned dollars to work, then you need this book.

Compared to other types of investments, real estate ranks as one of the most profitable, least risky, and most stable choices (though, if part of the fun of investing is a rollercoaster-like risk, there are real estate investments for you, too). No matter what's going on in the world, people need a place to live and somewhere to work, and that means real estate will always be in demand, making it a perfect piece for every portfolio.

When you hear the phrase "real estate investing," the first thing to come to mind may be renting properties to tenants. Or perhaps you may think of house flipping, something which has become increasingly popular. While these are certainly types of real estate investing, they're far from the only ones. Among the kinds of real estate investing to choose from are:

• Tax Liens and Tax Deeds
• Foreclosures
• Notes
• Syndications

In this book, you'll learn about all of these and more. You'll discover how to take advantage of special tax breaks, choose the most profitable investment methods, and even how to participate in large projects with little money.

If you are looking for passive-income streams with high yields in relatively low-risk enterprises, or if you just want to dip your toes to make some money on the side, this book will serve as a reliable guide.

Chapter 1: A Powerful Combination

"Compound interest is the most powerful force in the universe. He who understands it, earns it. He who doesn't, pays it."

\- Albert Einstein

Retirement accounts with their tax advantages and their built-in compound returns are great investment tools that, when combined with real estate, will create a powerful, synergetic wealth creation machine to propel your net worth much higher than other alternatives.

1.1 Real Estate Investing

Real estate investing is a time-tested way to build wealth. Even the passive income made by owning and renting property has proven better than investing in the stock market.

While the stock market and renting can have similar returns (between 8% and 12% a year), real estate has the potential for appreciation and certain tax advantages that make it better for wealth creation and retention. On the other hand, investment retirement accounts (IRAs) are also a great way to save money for retirement as they provide huge tax advantages and a great way to accumulate wealth.

Even small investments made early on can generate huge returns thanks to compound interest, the "most powerful force in the universe."

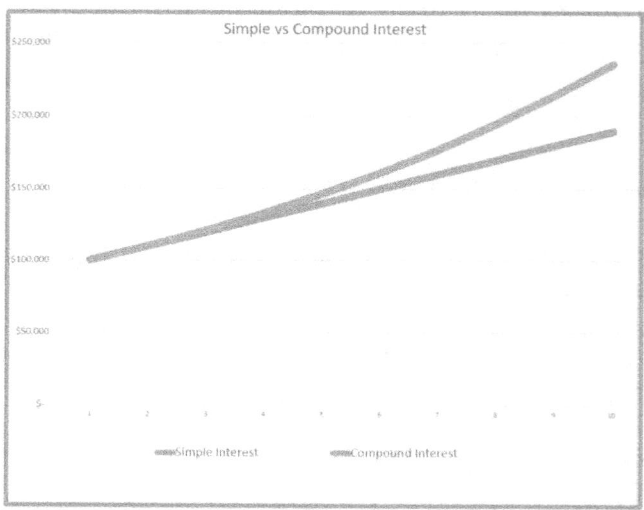

Simple vs. Compound Interest

Considering that land possession was once the definition of wealth, real estate has been the vehicle used for wealth creation for the longest time. It not only can generate income, but can retain that income as well.

Real estate will preserve its value in good times and bad, as it's less subject to the up and downs of the stock market. A mom-and-pop operator of rentals will beat the S&P 500, and even the real estate exchange-traded funds (ETFs) every time because they don't have the overhead and they are much more careful where they invest.

Even Warren Buffet, the "Oracle of Omaha" and the undisputed investment wizard, said that he'd buy up "a couple hundred thousand" single-family homes if it were practical to do so.

If held for long enough and purchased at low rates, Buffett says houses are even better than stocks. He advises buyers to take out a 30-year mortgage and refinance if rates go down.

Even though Buffet's Berkshire Hathaway is not buying houses, other funds are. A big one is Blackstone, a major investment firm that traditionally has invested in the stock market and is now buying single-family residential houses (SFR) by the thousands. Some other major funds are also buying houses to rent. They are entering the business in droves because there is money to be made.

But real estate is not just renting, or "buy and hold," as it is referred to in the industry. Other investment types can be made, which we'll discuss later on. However, because we are dealing with IRS-regulated retirement accounts, we are only going to talk about passive investments.

Let's start by defining passive: A passive investment is one where the investor provides the capital and has no say on how the entity that uses the money will operate. The investor is not actively involved in the running of the business using the money.

There is also the Internal Revenue Service (IRS) definition of passive investment, which is important for the tax implications of the investment. According to the IRS, passive investments are defined as above but also include renting and any other investments in which the taxpayer does not have material participation.

Material participation is further defined as:

- If the investor dedicates more than 500 hours to a business or activity from which you're profiting.

- If the participation in an activity has been "substantially all" of the participation for that tax year.

- If the participation is up to 100 hours, and that is at least as much as any other person involved in the activity.

Passive real estate investing does include holding notes secured by real estate, "buy and hold," and buy and sell if held for at least a year.

Let's not forget that a key to high long-term results is diversification and self-directed Individual retirement accounts provide a way to diversify into real estate and other assets as opposed to just stocks and bonds that are, by far, the most often used vehicles in retirement accounts.

1.2 Retirement Accounts

There are several vehicles for retirement accounts: 401(k), individual retirement accounts (IRAs), Roth IRAs, and others.

Among those retirement accounts, there is a lesser-known account type called a self-directed individual retirement account (SDIRA), which allows a retirement account—with all of its tax advantages—to invest in real estate with its great returns.

The traditional investment vehicle for most of these accounts is the stock market where you invest in bonds and stocks.

One of the greatest benefits of retirement accounts is that their earnings are not taxed while you keep the money in the account, allowing for a greater rate of re-investment and getting the benefit of compound interest.

Compound interest is the interest you earn on both the principal amount and the interest earned on the principal.

For example: let's say you have $1,000 and you earn 10% for a $100 return. The power of compound interest is that on the next cycle, you now earn 10% on $1,100 for a $110 return—and on and on it goes.

Time is the most important factor when it comes to compound returns, and it's your most powerful ally. Because an IRA is established for long-term use and will not be used until retirement, your funds will compound with each succeeding investment.

Compounding returns is an extremely powerful concept, but investors often fail to account for taxation when performing these compounding calculations. If we remove the variable of taxation from your compounding calculation, you will see that you can accelerate the accumulation of wealth. And how can you eliminate this variable of taxation, you ask? Simply by using a self-directed IRA or another tax-advantaged investment account.

A self-directed IRA gives you the power to invest outside the stock market. You can invest in several passive investment types that can give you a better return.

In 2012, the Securities and Exchange Commission estimated about 2% of IRAs were self-directed. At the time, this would have equated to about $100 billion in assets. The use of SDIRAs has continued to increase, especially after the 2008 crash and the stock market slump that followed. Also, the financial impact of the COVID-19 pandemic has created more interest in investing in real Estate

Not only are investors putting more money into alternative asset classes, but they are increasingly trusting to do so in self-directed IRAs.

1.3 IRA + Real Estate – An Overview

You can combine the tax deferral and compound returns benefits of retirement accounts with the wealth-building prowess of real estate.
You do this by using a self-directed IRA (SDIRA) to hold Real Estate investments.

To get started, you need to move your 401k, form a prior employer, or a current IRA account to a custodian of SDIRA accounts.   Once your money is there, you constitute a Limited Liability Company (LLC) where your IRA account is the member and you are the manager.

At this point, you need to open a checking account in some bank.   You then instruct your IRA custodian to purchase the LLC with your funds.   The custodian will send the LLC a check that you can deposit in the LLC account and now you can direct that money to buy real estate or to invest in several other businesses.

You must keep meticulous track of the money for the LLC and make sure you don't mix it with your funds. You also have to keep in mind that any gains you make have to go back to the LLC account and if you want to expend the money outside investing, you must go through a formal distribution process out of your IRA account.

All this and more are explained in the following chapters.

Chapter 2: The Different Types of Retirement Accounts

"How many millionaires do you know who have become wealthy by investing in savings accounts? I rest my case."

- Robert G. Allen

2.1 The Changing Retirement Accounts

Retirement accounts have evolved since Congress created the original (or traditional) IRA. New types of IRAs were added, and eligibility and contribution rules have been updated several times.

In 1978, Congress established the Simplified Employee Pension (SEP) IRA, an employer-based IRA. Between 1982 and 1986, Congress made the traditional IRA available to all workers under age of 70½, expanding the eligibility beyond those who were not covered by an employer plan and allowing anyone with earned income to make tax-deductible IRA contributions.

Beginning in 1987, Congress eliminated the universality of tax-deductible IRA contributions but permitted workers meeting certain income limits to make such contributions, even if they were covered by employer-sponsored retirement plans. In addition, after-tax (or nondeductible) contributions were permitted. In 1996, Congress added the Savings Incentive Match Plan for Employees (SIMPLE IRA), an account targeted at small businesses.

Throughout the 1990s, additional changes were made to the IRA, including adjustments to spousal IRAs and income limitations. The biggest change was the introduction of the Roth IRA in 1997. The Roth IRA has revolutionized the IRA market and provided additional tax benefits regarding growth to allow individuals to keep their earnings tax-free. Contribution limits have periodically increased since the inception of the IRA, making way for more meaningful annual contributions.

With each adjustment to the IRA, new opportunities for investors have emerged. The IRA might still evolve as more individuals realize they must take retirement into their own hands rather than rely on employers or the government.

To decide which type of IRA is right for you, you must first determine how the invested funds will be taxed. Reviewing these accounts and their differences will enable you to select the account that will meet your needs in the most tax-efficient way.

When you hear the term "self-directed," as it refers to IRAs, 401(k)s, and other retirement accounts, don't be thrown off. Self-directed simply refers to the freedom you have with your account. The large majority of banks and custodians limit your IRA investments to traditional investments and with the SDIRA you branch out to many other kinds of investments.

We will first review the individual account types before moving into qualified plans available to small business owners, and then we'll conclude with special accounts that help to reduce healthcare and education costs. You will notice many accounts have both a traditional and a Roth account type, which is an important distinction to understand.

2.2 Traditional IRA

When an employee puts money away for retirement, it is set aside in a 401(k), 403(b), or another similar program that provides a way to save money for retirement through an employer plan.

When an employee changes jobs, they can no longer contribute to the company account, and so one option may be to "roll over" the funds into another qualified retirement plan, such as an IRA.

Individuals can also open an IRA to set money aside for their retirement needs when they don't have access to a 401(k) or prefer to do so over a 401(k).

The IRA account is normally kept at a financial institution authorized to hold IRA accounts, such as companies like Vanguard, Merrill Lynch, and a myriad of others.

Through those institutions, the IRA funds are invested in stocks, bonds, and mutual funds. This is done because those companies are agents for the stock market, and they use these IRA accounts to feed their business.

The traditional IRA is an account with three key features:

1) Contributions are tax-deductible as long as requirements are met, meaning you could potentially reduce your current tax liability with annual contributions.

2) The funds in the account will grow tax-deferred, meaning they grow within the account without tax until they are withdrawn or taken as distributions.

3) When the money is withdrawn, it will be taxed as ordinary income. In other words, it will be taxed at the rate your income is taxed. Although the money is taxed on the way out of the account, owners are often in a lower tax bracket at that point in their life and still benefit from the tax-advantaged compounded growth they had received investing in their IRA.

This retirement account dictates that the funds must remain in the account until the account owner is 59½. If they are withdrawn before that time, they will be taxed and may be charged an additional 10% penalty for premature withdrawal, unless it is on the IRS list of exceptions. Contributions cannot be made beyond the age of 70½, at which time mandatory withdrawals are required each year. These withdrawals are commonly referred to as required minimum distributions (RMDs).

You can fund an IRA through three different methods: rollovers, transfers, and annual contributions. A rollover transfers funds from an employer-sponsored retirement account such as a 401(k), 403(b), 457, TSP, etc., into an IRA. Many workers do this when they change jobs. Rolling over a 401(k) to a self-directed IRA benefits the individual by increasing the available investment options from a dozen mutual funds and company stocks to an array of both traditional and alternative investments. It also reduces the expenses, as 401(k) fees are generally higher than IRA fees and their accompanying investments.

IRAs and cash within the accounts can also be transferred from one custodian to another. These transfers are generally sent directly from an existing custodian to the new custodian, without the account owner handling the funds. Assuming a direct trustee-to-trustee transfer, or a rollover occurs from one like-account to another, there is no tax liability for either a transfer or a rollover, and they do not impact the individual annual "out-of-pocket" contribution limits in the year the transfer is made.

Non-working spouses can make contributions under a special provision in the IRS rules. If the account owner is over age 50, an additional $1,000 can be added to the contribution each year. The household income will determine if the contribution amount is tax-deductible or not. Contribution limits may change from year-to-year and are tied to the rate of inflation.

You can set up and make contributions to a traditional IRA if you meet both of these requirements:

- You (or if you file a joint return, your spouse) received taxable compensation during the year.

- You were not yet 70½ years old by the end of the year.

If both you and your spouse have compensation and are under the age of 70½, each of you can set up an IRA. You cannot, however, both participate in the same IRA.

Compensation is defined as: the wages, salaries, commissions, bonuses, alimony, and any other amount that you receive for providing personal services. For individuals who are self-employed, sole proprietors, or partners in a partnership, "earned income" is another term for compensation. Passive income such as interest, dividends, and most rental income are not considered compensation for the purpose of funding an IRA.

Excess contributions receive a yearly excise tax of 6%. Excess contributions occur when more money is added to an IRA than is allowed. Each year the IRS publishes the contribution limits for each type of retirement account, occasionally raising the limits to account for inflation. If you contribute more than the allowable amount in a given year, you will be penalized 6% of the excess amount that remains in your IRA when your tax return is due.

It is important to keep in mind that the contribution limits apply to all IRAs you hold. Please check on the IRS website for the current limits on IRA contributions for the year as they change every year.

2.3 Roth IRA

Senator William V. Roth introduced the Roth IRA to U.S. retirement savers in 1997. The Roth is similar to the traditional IRA, but with one notable difference: the investment profits in a Roth IRA are tax-free.

The difference between traditional and Roth accounts is important to understand because most investors must choose between the two when electing to make their contributions. The Roth IRA contributions do not offer a tax deduction in the year the funds are deposited. In exchange, the after-tax dollars grow tax-free and all money taken out of the account is tax-free, assuming account requirements are met.

Because contributions are made with money that has already been taxed, the amount you have contributed (excluding earnings) can be withdrawn at any time without early withdrawal penalties after the account has been established for five years. All profits and growth are required to be left in the account until the account owner is 59½ years old and the account has been established for five years or longer. These requirements help to protect their tax-free growth and encourage retirement savings.

You can contribute to your Roth IRA regardless of your age and can also contribute to a Roth IRA for your spouse. Contributions can be made through a 401(k) rollover, a custodian transfer, or annual contributions, much like the traditional IRA.

The annual contribution limits are the same as the traditional IRA, and an account owner can make combined contributions between both a traditional and Roth IRA, if desired. The total contributions to both accounts cannot exceed the annual contribution limits provided by the IRS.

You must meet the modified adjusted gross income (MAGI) limits to be eligible to invest and/or contribute to a Roth IRA. This may disqualify high-income earners from directly contributing to the Roth IRA. Fortunately, rollover contributions do not have the income restrictions that apply to direct (out-of-pocket) contributions, so you may still be able to transfer an existing plan into a Roth IRA.

Additionally, if you do not qualify to directly contribute to a Roth IRA, you may still be able to fund a traditional IRA and execute a Roth conversion so the funds can still be available for tax-free growth by way of your investments. It is important to consult with a tax professional, CPA, or financial advisor when considering these options.

One of the main benefits of a self-directed Roth IRA is that there is no required minimum distribution at 70½ years old, and you can continue to contribute as long as you have earned income while still maintaining tax-free withdrawals. Additionally, you may be able to pass along your Roth IRA earnings to beneficiaries tax-free so they can also benefit from the tax-free savings you've accumulated.

When you roll over a 401(k) or IRA, it will be transferred under the same structure as the existing account. This means if you roll over a traditional 401(k), it will become a traditional IRA and the tax treatment will remain the same (tax-deferred). In the same manner, a Roth 401(k) will roll over into a Roth IRA with the same tax-free treatment.

As of 2022, you can rollover accounts from 401(k)s directly into their Roth counterparts as well as traditional IRAs to Roth IRAs via a Roth conversion. It is important to seek tax advice for either of these transactions as the amount of the rollover may be taxed in the year of the conversion. Many investors still find this an attractive option because of the tax-free growth capability.

When deciding between the traditional or Roth account options, you should ask yourself, "Would I rather pay taxes on the seed, or would I rather pay taxes down the road when I harvest the crop?"

A traditional IRA allows you to deduct your contribution amounts from your taxable income, thus reducing your tax liability for that year. Since it is a tax-deferred account, you can reinvest your money and grow it faster than if the investment gains were taxed, but with the understanding that when you remove the money from your account, you will have to pay taxes—that is, you are deciding to defer your taxes until the harvest.

On the other hand, Roth accounts are taxed on the seed, or when you put money into your account. While you might not see the benefit instantaneously when you turn that $5,000 into $15,000, the additional $15,000 you just earned will never be taxed. When the harvest comes, what you've cultivated is yours and not Uncle Sam's. It is important to consider your unique situation and retirement goals, and to consult with a trusted tax accountant or tax advisor when making these decisions.

2.4 Traditional 401(k) and Roth 401(k)

The traditional 401(k) is a savings plan offered to employees that allows them to set aside tax-deferred income for retirement. The 401(k) is attractive to employers and employees because of the high contribution amounts and large tax deductions available.

The Roth 401(k) possesses the same benefits as the 401(k), but with the ability to designate a portion of funds as Roth contributions. Roth contributions may be withdrawn tax- and penalty-free as long as the participant is at least 59½ years of age and has held the account for at least five years. Investors don't have to worry about income limits and they still receive tax treatment similar to a Roth IRA.

This plan is available to anyone with a 401(k) and is a benefit to higher-paid employees and self-employed individuals who may have been excluded from having a Roth IRA because of income limitations. Contributions to a Roth 401(k) are irrevocable, meaning once the money goes into the account, participants may not later decide to move the funds into a regular tax-deferred account.

The Roth 401(k) has the same distribution requirements as the Traditional 401(k) and participants must begin taking minimum distributions by 70½ years old, which contrasts with the requirements for the Roth IRA. Account holders can often avoid this distribution requirement by rolling over their account into a Roth IRA.

2.5 Small Business Account Types

Whether you know it or not, you may be eligible for government-sponsored small business retirement plans such as the SIMPLE IRA, SEP IRA, Solo 401(k), and Roth Solo 401(k). Being an investor often qualifies you as self-employed, a sole proprietor, or even as your own small business.

The advantages of a self-directed SIMPLE, SEP, Solo 401(k), and Roth Solo 401(k) plan over a traditional or Roth IRA are clear: higher contribution limits and larger tax deductions. In addition, you can contribute to both an individual account (such as a traditional or Roth IRA) *and* a small business plan in order to truly maximize the investing power of your self-directed retirement accounts.

It's important to know the basic facts about each plan before making an investment decision that will impact your future. The following is a brief overview of the SIMPLE, SEP, Solo 401(k), and Roth Solo 401(k):

2.6 Simplified Employee Pension (SEP) IRA

This is a retirement account that is available to small business owners who typically employ fewer than 25 employees and allows individuals to make contributions toward their retirement without getting involved in a more complex qualified plan such as a 401(k). Any employer (whether a corporation, partnership, or self-employed individual) may establish the plan, even if there's only one employee.

The SEP IRA operates much like a traditional IRA in that the contributions are tax-deductible to the business, the earnings grow tax-deferred, money cannot be withdrawn without penalty until the account owner is 59½ years old, and withdrawals are taxed as ordinary income. SEP IRA owners are also required to make RMDs when they turn 70½. Small business owners like these plans because they are simple to set up and are a cost-effective way to plan for retirement.

The advantage of a SEP IRA over a traditional IRA is that the contribution limits are much higher. An account owner can contribute up to 25% of the earned income of each employee (up to $61,000 per year), compared to the $6,000 limit for the IRA (for 2022). This plan is an employer contribution plan and employees cannot contribute directly. The plan must cover all employees who earn at least $550, are at least 21 years of age, and have worked for the employer for three of the last five years. For a full list of exemptions, consult with your tax advisor or visit the IRS website.

2.7 SIMPLE IRA

SIMPLE IRA stands for Savings Incentive Match Plan for Employees Individual Retirement Account.
A SIMPLE IRA is another plan option for small business owners and is popular with investors who pay themselves $45,000 or less. It's an incentive-match plan designed for small businesses with 100 or fewer employees that have no other qualified plan. With a SIMPLE IRA, an employer contributes a percent-based salary match to its employees' SIMPLE IRAs, while the employees make elective salary deferrals. The basic framework of this account is similar to a Traditional 401(k) or IRA with the same tax deduction, tax deferment, and withdrawal rules.

The SIMPLE IRA was designed specifically to help small business owners (you, if you're self-employed or a sole proprietor) offer a retirement plan to their employees. The main advantage of this plan is that the account balances compound tax-deferred until funds are withdrawn. Plus, an employee can contribute 100% of his or her annual compensation, up to a maximum of $14,000 for those under the age of 50 and $17,000 for those employees over the age of 50 (for 2022).

Employers are generally required to provide a company match rather than a set contribution amount to all employees. If the employee does not contribute with his or her own funds, the employer is not required to contribute to that employee's account.

You can set up a SIMPLE IRA plan if you meet both of the following requirements:

- You meet the employee limit.

- You do not maintain another qualified plan unless the other plan is for collective bargaining employees.

2.8 Solo 401(k) and Roth Solo 401(k)

The Solo 401(k) is often the most attractive plan to investors—if they qualify—because it combines elements of both the SEP and SIMPLE. This plan is designed for owner-only businesses and spouses. It can be established by both incorporated and unincorporated businesses, sole proprietorships, partnerships, and corporations. You can contribute annually through salary deferral, plus a profit-sharing portion of up to 25 % of your salary.

The Solo 401(k) is derived from the 401(k) plan. The only difference is that the Solo 401(k) was designed for owner-only businesses and spouses, while the 401(k) plan is sponsored by companies with multiple employees. The Solo 401(k) plan must be the only plan maintained by the business and the business can't be considered part of a controlled group under tax law.

The total Solo 401(k) contribution limit is up to $58,000 in 2021 and $61,000 in 2022. There is a catch-up contribution of an extra $6,500 for those 50 or older.

To understand Solo 401(k) contribution rules, you want to think of yourself as two people: an employer (of yourself) and an employee (yes, also of yourself). Within that overall $58,000 contribution limit in 2021 and $61,000 in 2022, your contributions are subject to additional limits in each role:

- As the employee, you can contribute up to $19,500 in 2021 and $20,500 in 2022, or 100% of compensation, whichever is less. Those 50 or older get to contribute an additional $6,500 here.

- As the employer, you can make an additional profit-sharing contribution of up to 25% of your compensation or net self-employment income. The limit on compensation that can be used to factor your contribution is $290,000 in 2021 and $305,000 in 2022.

Would you like the same benefits of the Solo 401(k) but with the tax benefits of Roth-type contributions? Consider the Roth Solo 401(k).

In 2006, Congress merged two of the most popular types of retirement savings plans: the Roth IRA and the Solo 401(k) into a Roth Solo 401(k). The Roth Solo 401(k) possesses the same benefits as the Solo 401(k), but with the tax benefits of Roth-type contributions. If you want Roth tax advantages (tax-free distributions) with a substantial contribution limit, then the Roth Solo 401(k) is for you.

Also, if you are interested in a Roth IRA, but you don't qualify because of income limits, then the Roth Solo 401(k) is an option to consider. The same contribution limits apply as the traditional Solo 401(k), but you can designate the salary deferral contributions you make as Roth contributions. The portion you contribute does not qualify for a tax deduction, but the profits from these contributions grow tax-free, plus all qualified distributions are tax-free. The profit-sharing portion (0-25% of your salary) of the Roth Solo 401(k) is just like the traditional Solo 401(k) and is tax-deferred.

The advantages of a traditional or Roth Solo 401(k) plan over a traditional or Roth IRA are clear: much higher contribution limits and larger tax deductions. It truly is the most powerful retirement plan you have at your disposal.

Chapter 3: The Power of Self-Directed Accounts

3.1 Self-Directed IRA (SDIRA)

A Self Directed Individual Retirement Account, (SDIRA), works like an IRA but the SDIRA gives you a greater selection of types of investments that you can hold in the account.

Regular IRAs are limited to common securities like stocks, bonds, certificates of deposit, ETFs and mutual funds, whereas SDIRAs allows the owner to invest in a much more diverse array of assets. With an SDIRA, you can hold real estate, gold, commodities, private placements, limited partnerships, tax lien certificates, and other sorts of alternative investments.

3.2 Traditional vs. Roth SDIRA

Self-directed IRAs can be set up as traditional IRAs or as Roth IRAs. But they have different tax treatment, eligibility requirements, contribution guidelines, and distribution rules.

A key difference between a traditional and Roth IRA is when you pay the taxes. With traditional IRAs, you get an upfront tax break, but pay taxes on your contributions and earnings as you withdraw them during retirement. On the other hand, you don't get a tax break when you contribute to a Roth IRA, but your contributions and earnings grow tax-free, and qualified distributions are tax-free as well.

Of course, there are other differences to consider. Here's a quick rundown:

Income limits: There are no income limits for traditional IRAs, but you must make less than a certain amount to open or contribute to a Roth.

Required minimum distributions (RMDs): You must start taking RMDs at 72 years old if you have a traditional IRA. Roth IRAs have no RMDs during your lifetime.

Early withdrawals: With a Roth IRA, you can withdraw your contributions at any time, for any reason, with no incurred tax or penalty after the age of 59½, provided the account is at least five years old.

With traditional IRAs, withdrawals are similarly penalty-free starting at age 59½. Remember, you have to pay taxes on traditional IRA withdrawals. These same rules apply to whichever version of a self-directed IRA you have. SDIRAs also have to abide by the general IRA annual contribution limits. For 2021 and 2022, that's $6,000 per year, or $7,000 if you're age 50 or older.

3.3 Investing in a SDIRA

Self-directed Roth IRAs open up a large universe of potential investments. In addition to the standard investments (stocks, bonds, cash, money market funds, and mutual funds), you can hold assets that aren't typically part of a retirement portfolio.

For example, you can buy investment real estate to hold in your SDIRA account. You can also hold partnerships and tax liens, or even a franchise business.

The Internal Revenue Service (IRS) forbids a few specified investments in self-directed IRAs, whether it's a Roth or traditional version. For example, you can't hold life insurance, Stocks from S-corporation stock, and collectibles, which includes a wide range of items, such as: antiques, artwork, alcoholic beverages, baseball cards, memorabilia, jewelry, stamps, and rare coins (Gold is allowed but not as rare gold coins).

3.4 Benefits of Self-Directed IRAs

Investor control is one of the most attractive features of self-directed IRAs. Investors can move in and out of investments as they see fit. With the proper tools, they can evaluate each investment, its risks, potential returns, and the time horizon that the money will be invested. Self-directed IRAs provide tremendous flexibility and allow investors to hand-select investments that not only meet their portfolio needs but are also within their comfort level.

No longer must investors be subject to the whims of an unstable market, not knowing if and how much of a return they might receive. Investing money into an account and hoping that the markets do not decline around the time the funds are needed can be very stressful. The ability to evaluate and make decisions with an understanding of the investment from the outset can bring peace of mind and a greater sense of control.

Why rely solely on the stock market, especially if you don't have expertise in that area when it's possible to invest in assets you know and understand? Combining your expertise and the advantages of an IRA's tax-deferred or tax-free growth can be a powerful investment strategy that allows you to capitalize on the benefits discussed in the following sections.

Tax savings are one of the key reasons investors use self-directed IRAs rather than investing in the same instruments outside of an IRA. Tax savings will either be tax-deferred or tax-free, depending on the type of account that has been established. Either option will provide compounded growth faster than in accounts that are taxed each year. Plus, in tax-deferred accounts, you may be eligible for a tax deduction on annual contributions, thus reducing the amount you pay in taxes that year.

Asset protection and generational wealth building are two additional benefits self-directed IRAs provide. IRAs are afforded protection under federal bankruptcy law, and thus generally are shielded from creditors in bankruptcy proceedings. Consult a tax attorney for further guidance on this topic.

Additionally, certain IRAs allow assets to be passed on to beneficiaries while largely avoiding probate and taxes. Self-directed IRAs can benefit your family's financial future with estate planning that leaves valuable IRA assets to loved ones without the burden of taxes.

Where to Invest? Understanding the "Why" and "How" First

Where or what you will invest in is not nearly as important as understanding how and why. It is not necessary to have an alternative investment in mind before establishing a self-directed IRA because when you open an account you are opening the door to take advantage of opportunities as they occur.

Many alternative investment opportunities come and go quickly. If you are not prepared to act on the opportunity, there will be others who will recognize its value and they will be the ones to invest. It is always better to have an open door than a closed one.

It takes time to set up the SDIRA, so you may want to get going with that as you do your research and pick the kind of investments you want to make.

If you know how you would like to invest (in a tax-advantaged retirement account) and why (to take advantage of compound interest, tax savings, asset protection, and the ability to raise tax-advantaged money for investments you know and understand), then you are already in a position to take advantage whenever the "where" comes about. Allowing time to research opportunities and understand the investment thoroughly will always provide the best scenario for success.

Fortunately, self-directed IRAs do not require an all-or-nothing approach. It is possible to invest a portion of your retirement funds in a self-directed account while leaving other funds in traditional investments. This will allow you to gain knowledge and become comfortable with the various alternative investment opportunities and the self-directed IRA investment process. Many investors start out self-directing a small percentage of their portfolios into alternatives and gradually allocate a greater percentage of their overall portfolios into their self-directed account as they find success and gain more confidence.

Often investors are told that it is not possible to invest their IRA in real estate or other alternative assets. You may still encounter CPAs, banks, and other financial professionals who are not aware of the opportunities available with self-directed IRAs. This is merely due to an education gap. For this reason, it is important to get the wheels in motion sooner than later to be in a good position when the time comes.

3.5 How does the SDIRA operate?

With most IRA providers, you can only open a regular IRA (traditional or Roth), and can only invest in the usual suspects of stocks, bonds, and mutual funds/ETFs. If you want to open a self-directed IRA, you'll need a qualified IRA custodian that specializes in that type of account. However, not every SDIRA custodian offers the same range of investments. So if you're interested in a specific asset, such as gold bullion, make sure it's part of a potential custodian's offerings.

Remember that SDIRAs are self-directed, which means custodians aren't allowed to give financial advice. As such, traditional brokerages, banks, and investment companies usually don't offer them to their clients. This means you need to do your homework. If you need help picking or managing your investments, you should plan on working with a financial advisor.

As we discussed earlier, there are three ways to fund a self-directed IRA. You can make annual contributions to the traditional or Roth IRA. This contribution can be made every year going forward. CESAs, small-business retirement accounts, and HSAs all have different contribution limits as previously discussed.

If you have IRA funds with another institution, you can transfer some or all of those funds into a self-directed IRA. This will be a custodian-to-custodian transfer. If you are not sent a check, there is no IRS reporting necessary and no tax consequences to the transaction. If you choose to have the check mailed to you and take active receipt of the funds, you have a 60-day window to return the funds to a qualified plan. If you miss the window, there may be taxes and penalties owed and it will be considered a withdrawal. This is referred to as a 60-day rollover and you are only permitted to perform this once in a 12-month running period across all plans in your name.

Rollovers can be completed from 401(k) plans with former employers. This process will be dictated by the former employer and if you elect this method, we can walk you through the process. In this case, often the previous custodian of the 401(k) will issue the individual a check, at which point it is important to deposit it immediately as the same 60-day rules apply.

The last of the account open options is a conversion. This includes taking a traditional IRA (or other tax-deferred account) and converting it to a Roth IRA.

As the rules have recently changed, this has become a transaction that is in high demand. This transaction triggers initial tax consequences and may not be available to everyone due to income limitations. Meeting with a tax advisor or financial planner before a planned conversion is recommended to help minimize taxes and understand the financial consequences of the transfer. For many, taking a tax hit one year in exchange for tax-free growth over the next several decades makes sense, although you'll want to understand all your options before completing a conversion.

It's possible to combine several account funding methods for your self-directed IRA. It is also important to remember that conversions and transfers do not count against your accounts' contribution limits each year.

By now you should be seeing the benefits a self-directed IRA has to offer. To take advantage of the tax savings, compounding interest, and the other benefits we've touched on, you must stay compliant with the IRS rules and regulations about these accounts.

The IRS does not specify what can be held inside of an IRA. Instead, they offer strict guidelines regarding what an IRA *cannot* invest. The IRS rules are more of an exclusive rather than inclusive list. The IRA owner takes responsibility for where funds are invested and what investments they deem appropriate for the account. The custodian follows the directions of the account owner and holds the tax status of the IRA. Therefore, you need to understand the IRS rules and prohibited transactions before investing.

Since the IRS provides a guide of *don'ts*, your opportunities are essentially only limited by your imagination, plus a few IRS specifics. This leaves a great deal of flexibility to invest in opportunities that align with your passions, experiences, and expertise.

Self-directed IRAs are treated much like a trust. The IRA is its own entity and is separate from the individual who owns the IRA. The IRA (the account) and the beneficiary (you) are two separate entities and must be kept separate with all transactions.

This exclusive benefit rule states that all transactions must be made for the exclusive benefit of the IRA and not the IRA owner. IRS rules state that when it comes to a self-directed IRA investment, you and the investment must be at arm's length. In other words, you can't directly benefit from an asset owned by the IRA. The IRA entity can benefit from the transactions, but not the IRA owner. Remember, the IRA is built to provide for your future and is not intended to benefit you now. It is considered an "indirect benefit" if your IRA is engaged in transactions that, in some way, can benefit you personally. This is strictly prohibited.

Some examples of indirect benefits include:

- Personally using your IRA property. Using real estate purchased through your IRA as an office, personal residence, vacation home, retirement home, etc., is not allowed.

- Receiving personal benefits from your IRA. You can't lend yourself money from your IRA. Moreover, you can't personally work on your investment property or pay yourself or a company that you own to do work on an investment owned by your IRA.

- Revenue and expenses must flow directly through the IRA. Since a self-directed IRA is for retirement, it's important to remember that all expenses related to an investment are paid from the IRA and all profits are returned to the IRA.

To provide a clearer understanding of the IRS rules and regulations, let's break each topic down specifically.

Disqualified assets include tangible personal property such as collectibles. This includes artwork, rugs, antiques, metals (except the precious metals discussed earlier), gems, stamps, coins, and alcoholic beverages. These are the prohibited transactions specifically listed under Title 26 of the Internal Revenue Code. Your IRA is allowed to invest in hedge funds or mutual funds that specialize in these items, but not to hold the specific items as a collection within the IRA.

Additionally, the IRA cannot invest in life insurance or S Corporations. The IRA can own businesses that are structured as a Limited Partnership (LP), an LLC, a C Corporation, or another entity as long as a disqualified person does not own more than 50% of the entity.

Disqualified individuals include you as the IRA owner, your spouse, and your ascendants or descendants. This includes your parents, grandparents, and great-grandparents as ascendants. It also includes your children, grandchildren, and great-grandchildren (and any of their spouses) as descendants.

Other disqualified individuals include those who have fiduciary responsibility over the IRA. This could include your custodian, an accountant that has power of attorney over the account, an attorney, CPA, financial advisor, or other individuals that have access and fiduciary responsibility over your IRA. IRS rules dictate that a self-directed IRA may not buy an investment from, sell to, or otherwise be involved with any disqualified person.

Aside from these exclusions, there is a wide range of people with whom your IRA can do business. Relatives such as brothers and sisters or aunts and uncles are not disqualified. Any third party, business partner, friend, business associate, and so forth are all eligible to buy or sell to and from the IRA. While transactions with non-linear relatives will not violate the disqualified person rule, if the transaction provides a benefit to a disqualified person, it will still be deemed a prohibited transaction.

In addition to disqualified persons, there can also be disqualified entities. This includes any businesses that have more than 50% ownership by a disqualified person.

Prohibited transactions include any improper use of your IRA by you, your beneficiary, or any disqualified person. Such activity could include disqualified persons borrowing money from the IRA, lending money to the IRA, selling or buying an asset to or from the IRA, receiving unreasonable compensation for managing the account, using the account as security for a loan, or buying a property with the account for personal use. Essentially, a disqualified person cannot be involved in any transaction, regardless of the actual result of the transaction. If the benefit was intended, even if the investment fails, it will be deemed a prohibited transaction based upon intent. Any benefit received is viewed by the IRS as self-dealing and results in a prohibited transaction.

Regarding prohibited transactions related to the use of the property, the account owner or any disqualified person cannot use any assets inside the IRA for their personal use. This would include a vacation home that serves as a rental property. The IRA owner cannot stay in or on the property, cannot use the property as security for a loan, and cannot receive unreasonable compensation for any transactions involved within the IRA.

If the investor chooses to rehabilitate property within the IRA, he or she cannot complete the work (or what is referred to by the IRS as "sweat equity") as this is considered to offer an immediate benefit to the account holder. Work must be contracted to a non-disqualified third party. However, it is acceptable to manage the property as long as no personal benefit is received. That said, paying bills, collecting rent, and directing the actions of the IRA are generally acceptable. Completing the paperwork, establishing leases, and contracting a third party for repairs also generally falls within the acceptable guidelines.

A common question arises concerning the ability to act as a real estate agent and be paid a commission. This would constitute a prohibited transaction because you, as the agent and IRA owner, would receive a personal benefit from the transaction. This would be considered self-dealing.

It is important to be very conservative when it comes to the self-dealing provision. For instance, if your IRA purchased raw land, you would be prohibited from hunting on that land with your friends. Even a one-time hunting trip could put your entire IRA at risk. Occasional attempts have been made to use what is termed a "straw person" to avoid prohibited transactions. The IRS considers these events a violation of the "step transaction doctrine," making them prohibited transactions.

Let's consider an example: If the real estate broker from the previous example wanted to receive the commission on a sale of his or her IRA property, he or she might consider adding a step in which a friend acts as a "straw person" and receives the commission from the IRA before passing it on to the IRA owner. While the IRA isn't directly paying the IRA owner the commission, the step transaction doctrine considers this an extra step added solely to circumvent the IRS tax code and so it would be deemed a prohibited transaction.

The second aspect of prohibited transactions is that the IRA owner must pay fair market value for any assets that are purchased. This is interpreted as buying an asset for the price the seller would sell to anyone in the existing market. The purpose of the rule is to prevent special treatment between a seller and the buyer. This concept is an expansion of the exclusive benefit rule.

For example, while your brother or sister may not be a disqualified person, it is still imperative that you conduct any transactions at fair market value. This demonstrates that you are not receiving an undue benefit of a discounted price (due to your relationship) that would not be available in the current market.

3.6 Distributions

Early distributions are generally penalized if they are taken before the age of 59½. (Distributions are also commonly referred to as withdrawals.) Your account will be assessed a 10% penalty and will have to pay taxes on the distributed amount at the ordinary income tax rate. This includes both traditional and Roth IRAs, along with business retirement accounts like the SEP and the SIMPLE IRA. The power of Roth IRAs is that you can withdraw funds that you have contributed to the account at any time without incurring tax after the account has been established for five years. It is the profits and account growth that is subject to the 59½ age requirements and early distribution penalties.

CESAs require distributions for qualified educational purposes rather than reaching a certain retirement age. Any distribution that is not used for a qualified education expense will be subject to a 10% penalty and will be taxed at the ordinary income tax rate. There are also penalties associated with the CESA account if the funds are not used by the beneficiary's 30th birthday. If the account is still funded when the beneficiary reaches the age of 30, the entire account balance will be distributed, assessed a 10% penalty, and taxed at the ordinary income tax rate.

Fortunately, CESAs allow the investor to change beneficiaries. For example, if you have two daughters and the first one reaches the age of 29 and does not plan to utilize the last $10,000 in her CESA, you can transfer the funds and make your younger daughter the account's beneficiary. Lastly, the HSA account will incur a 10%

penalty on any withdrawals not used for qualified health-related expenses.

Exceptions to the early withdrawal penalty for IRAs and retirement accounts include death or the permanent disability of the account owner. Other exceptions include: medical expenses or medical insurance within the exception guidelines; higher education expenses; the purchase of your first home; payment of an IRS Levy; or a distribution taken as an annuity in equal payments.

Required minimum distributions (also called mandatory withdrawals) impact traditional IRAs, SEP, and SIMPLE retirement accounts. At the age of 70½, the IRA owner must begin taking distributions from their accounts each year. The amount of the distribution is determined by IRS calculations and will result in penalties if a minimum distribution is not made. If all IRAs are held by the same custodian, the custodian will generally calculate the RMD for the account holder and send appropriate notifications regarding the RMD. If an investor owns IRAs held by different custodians, the account owner needs to communicate with each custodian to ensure the proper amounts are distributed each year.

Roth IRAs do not have mandatory withdrawals determined by age. The CESA accounts must be used for educational purposes by the 30th birthday of the beneficiary, or transferred to a new beneficiary while following IRS guidelines.

Penalties for non-compliance can be significant. If the IRS determines a prohibited transaction has occurred, even unintentionally, your entire account will lose its qualified tax-advantaged IRA status. This triggers a distribution of those funds from the IRA, resulting in taxes and penalties. Not only does the account lose its tax-advantaged status, but the funds are also taxed at your ordinary income-tax rate along with a 10% penalty. As you can see, it is critical to ensure you are conducting your self-directed IRA investments within the confines of the IRS rules and regulations.

With the flexibility self-directed IRAs provide, there is a wide range of investment transactions that can be completed without working in the gray area of the IRS code. Equity Trust strongly encourages clients to work firmly within the IRS rules and regulations so there is no question about the legitimacy of the transaction. With so few limitations, it is unwise to complete transactions that may have the potential to be considered a prohibited transaction or with a disqualified person. Regardless of the investment opportunity, the risk of losing your retirement savings is never worth it.

The self-directed IRA gives account owners a great deal of discretion. While the final decision is always yours, seeking education from Equity University or calling your senior account executive with questions is always encouraged. In addition, seeking counsel from your CPA, tax attorney, financial planner, or accountant experienced with the IRS rules regarding self-directed IRAs is the best way to avoid penalties.

When retirement finally arrives, it's time to begin living off the investments that you've cultivated over the years.

Sometimes it's difficult to move from the accumulation stage to the distribution stage because you have become accustomed to saving. But when the income stops, having a substantial nest egg to rely on for monthly bills and expenses is why you've saved up your account.

The best approach is to organize a plan when it is time to begin taking distributions. Consider all sources of income, what funds need to be available for distribution, and whether distributions will be received monthly, quarterly, or annually. Then schedule distributions based on your anticipated retirement budget. It is a good idea to have investments that continue to work for you during retirement rather than as cash waiting for a designated distribution date.

Many investors find success by changing their investment strategy rather than liquidating a significant portion of their investment portfolio. There are options for lending, tax lien investments, and rental property which can provide monthly cash flow options while the funds remain invested. These strategies can help your retirement funds last longer and create a legacy for your family in addition to ensuring that you do not outlive your money.

Distribution Rules

Before the age of 59½, any distribution made from an IRA is considered an early withdrawal and may be subject to taxes and penalties. There is a finite list of exceptions. If any of the following exceptions are met, the funds will not incur the 10% penalty, although taxes may be incurred depending on the type of account. Exceptions include:

- Death or permanent disability of the account holder. Distributions can be made to the beneficiary of the account.

- Continuous payments that are made based on the life expectancy of the account owner for at least five years, or until the account owner reaches 59½ years old. This exception establishes an annuity for the account holder with equal and periodic payments that are made at least annually.

- Payments made under a qualified domestic relations order (QDRO). This exception allows for retirement accounts to be settled and divided in the event of a divorce.

- Withdrawals for payments of medical care or the cost of insurance. For medical care, the medical expenses must be in an amount that is greater than the allowable medical expense deduction. The exception for insurance payments can cover expenses for insurance during periods of unemployment.

- Qualified educational expenses for CESA accounts.

- To buy, build, or rebuild a first home.

- Distributions due to an IRS levy.

- Distributions after the age of 59½.

(For a complete explanation of exceptions, see IRS Publication 590.)

As you've learned, there are two basic types of retirement accounts. The first is the tax-deferred account, such as a traditional IRA, SEP IRA, SIMPLE IRA, or traditional 401(k). The second account type is a Roth account, which is available as an IRA, 401(k), or Solo 401(k).

Traditional IRAs and similar tax-deferred accounts receive funds that are tax-deductible at the time of the contribution. They grow tax-deferred and incur taxes at the rate of ordinary income when distributions are taken. Roth IRAs do not receive a tax deduction at the time the contributions are made, but they grow tax-free and no taxes are due at the time of distribution.

Distribution Rules for Tax-Deferred Accounts

The taxes are incurred at the time of withdrawal when taking distributions from traditional accounts. As this creates a change in your tax situation, it is best to consult with your accountant or tax advisor regarding distributions. They will be able to consider all sources of income and advise a tax strategy that can keep the taxes to a minimum while providing the income necessary to meet your retirement needs.

The other important consideration with tax-deferred accounts is at the age of 70½, a required minimum distribution (RMD) is required. At this point, even if the funds are not needed, distributions must be taken from the account each year based on the account balance. The IRS has a distribution formula that is used to determine how much must be withdrawn each year.

If the IRA holder has more than one IRA, the RMD can be taken from any of the accounts. This becomes important if some accounts have more liquid assets than others. The full RMD may be taken from one account rather than having to liquidate an illiquid asset (such as real estate) held in another account. To accomplish this, the IRA owner must communicate with the IRA custodians so that the correct amount is distributed. If the full required distribution is not withdrawn, it may result in a 50% excise tax on the amount of RMD that was not taken.

Another step that must be completed each year is an assessment of the account value. When investments are in non-traditional investments, there may not be an obvious threshold (such as a monthly account statement) that establishes a value for the account. Therefore, it is up to the account holder to determine the value of the account.

Distribution Rules for Roth Accounts

Roth accounts are established with after-tax contributions, and thus they have the benefit of tax-free growth. The advantage is seen during the distribution phase. Many investors find that they can balance withdrawals from the Roth tax-free account and the tax-deferred accounts to minimize the taxes owed. A tax advisor is the best resource for establishing what options are most advantageous for your tax circumstances.

Roth account contributions can be withdrawn at any time with no tax consequences and without an early withdrawal penalty, regardless of age. However, withdrawing the money before retirement does not allow the account to grow over time, as it would if the funds remained in the account. If no exception exists, all profits that were earned must remain in the account until the owner is 59½ years old or they will be subject to early withdrawal penalties.

Another important feature of the Roth IRA is that it requires a five-year seasoning period, regardless of age. This means that if an investor opens an account at the age of 60, the account owner must wait until they're 65 to withdraw any gains without penalty.

A key advantage to the Roth IRA is that the funds will grow tax-free. Another is that there are no age limits on contributions or required minimum distributions like there are for the traditional IRA and other tax-deferred accounts. With a traditional IRA, no contributions can be made after the age of 70½ and withdrawals must begin at this time. With the Roth, neither one of these restrictions apply.

Establishing Adequate Income

Retirement is when all your hard work and financial planning come to fruition. It is time to set a retirement budget and determine where the income will come from. Meeting with a financial advisor can guide this decision-making process and tax advisors, accountants, and other retirement planners are also great resources. The process starts with determining your monthly cash flow needs, then reviewing your sources of income. You will need to determine when to take Social Security payments and what strategies can be used to maximize those payments. Social Security will likely provide the starting point for your income stream.

Evaluating other income streams outside of the retirement accounts might help to fill the gaps in your income needs. If you have passive income, such as a pension, interest payments, dividend income, CD income, or rental income, this will increase your cash flow. You should consider any income not inside your retirement accounts, but paid in regular intervals. At this point, you will have a clearer picture of how much money is coming in to replace your working income.

You may have a 401(k) from a former employer that can be rolled over into an IRA. As you plan, evaluate your total investment portfolio, how much can comfortably be withdrawn, and how long your money will last under the current investment structure. You shouldn't hold back in your planning and strategizing when it comes to withdrawals. The same due diligence and care that was used in finding great investments should also be employed here.

Consider spreading distributions over both tax-deferred and tax-free accounts, which may help to minimize taxes. Establish a strategy that will preserve the investments and extend them as long as possible while providing the income needs for your retirement. Often retirees can establish a strategy that will allow the bulk of the retirement funds to continue to grow while liquidating some funds to use on the fun stuff you laid out for yourself at the start of this book.

It is also important to consider potential unexpected expenses, such as healthcare costs, home repairs, travel expenses, and new hobbies that you might now have time to enjoy.

Planning for the distribution phase of retirement should be a meticulous but exciting process. Hopefully, you've been able to grow your portfolio over the years and, seeing the retirement you've dreamed of laid out in front of you, can now enjoy the fruits of your labor with a confident and well-thought-out strategy.

Chapter 4: Investing in Real Estate with an IRA

"Ninety percent of all millionaires become so through owning real estate. More money has been made in real estate than in all industrial investments combined. The wise young man or wage earner of today invests his money in real estate."

\- Andrew Carnegie, billionaire industrialist

4.1 Passive Investments

There are multiple investments that can be done in real estate. But to take full advantage of the tax benefits of using an SDIRA, several conditions must be met.

First off, the investment has to be passive, meaning you do not have material participation in the business. Somebody else or some company has to do the work. Passive investment includes investing in a corporation that itself conducts business and will pay taxes on its own before passing dividends to you. But again, if the business activity does pay taxes, then there is no tax advantage to you.

The only way to benefit from the no-tax advantage is through membership in a Limited Liability Corporation (LLC) that itself engages in passive investment. The LLC is a business structure that can be made transparent for tax purposes and the LLC itself does not pay taxes. It passes along the tax liability to the members, but since the member is an IRA, there are no taxes to pay.

For the SDIRA account that is invested in an LLC, the activity of the LLC must be passive. Otherwise, the SDIRA is liable for unrelated business income tax, which can be as high as 35%, and that makes it prohibitive.

You will think that you might be reduced to very limited options, but that is not the case. The following real estate activities are considered passive:

- Renting
- Notes
- Tax Liens

The following real estate related activities are considered passive if the property is held for over a year:

- Foreclosure investment
- Tax Deed investment
- Raw Land Subdivision
- Syndications and LLCs that buy and sell properties

In the following chapters, we'll explore each investment option and its tax treatment under an SDIRA.

4.2 Rental Properties

"Landlords grow rich in their sleep without working, risking or economizing."

\- John Stuart Mill, political economist

We'll start with renting as it is the most popular way to invest in real estate. Rental property investing is all about cash flow. You must be able to secure a positive cash flow while paying a mortgage, insurance, taxes, and repairs. This is especially true when investing in an IRA. You must be able to pay all expenses from the IRA, ideally through the income (rent) received from the property.

Rental investments can provide steady income and can be a fantastic investment for those reaching retirement age or looking for additional streams of income. Creating residual income has become a popular topic among investment circles. Residual income is income that comes in regularly without requiring a lot of additional work to generate the income.

Should you use your IRA, remember that the cash flow should flow to the IRA account. To use the money, you would have to do a withdrawal that will have tax consequences.

Rental Properties

Rental investments come in two primary forms: the first as long-term rentals (typically with a one- or two-year lease) and the second as short-term rentals for work or vacation.

There are important distinctions, benefits, and risks to each type of rental investment. Long-term rentals have a lower operating cost, given that the tenant will generally pay additional home costs such as utilities. There is often less ongoing maintenance, such as lawn care or basic upkeep of the home, which the renter generally provides depending on the lease agreement. Along with lower operating costs, income can be easier to predict which can help to manage costs more effectively. There are also lower management fees due to the single-tenant feature as opposed to the management of an apartment complex.

Short-term rentals can provide a higher weekly return (often close to what is collected for a monthly rental), but will also have a higher percentage of time the property is empty, depending on the location. These properties are typically located in a popular tourist or vacation destination and have the amenities that vacationers are looking for. This can include views, proximity to activities, and features like hot tubs and pools.

Short-term rentals also have higher maintenance costs. Utilities must remain on, and the costs of homeowner's dues, pools, or other amenities must be considered. It may be necessary to have a maintenance person on call along with a reliable housekeeper that can clean the property between renters. As a result, management companies are often used to manage short-term rental properties. However, due to the higher operating costs, property management fees for weekly rentals can eat into the return from rental income.

Investor cash flow is critical to successful rentals and should be carefully considered. Higher management fees can impact the ability to create positive cash flow. This is especially true if financing is a part of the expense equation.

The Business of Rental Property

The goal of investing in rental properties is to create a positive cash flow each month. To accurately access annual costs, many factors must be taken in account.

First is the cost of ownership. What is the monthly carrying cost of the property? Add taxes and insurance payments that must be paid each year and add the costs of upgrades or repairs. It is a good idea to set aside an additional budget for expected and unexpected repairs and maintenance.

Another important consideration is deciding if you will manage the property or if you will hire a property management company. If you are planning on investing in a rental property with your IRA, it's important to ensure you are following the IRS rules and regulations, which will add a layer of decision-making when considering the factors discussed above.

What will those costs be? Research must be completed on the rental rates for the neighborhood as well as the occupancy rates. If there are a lot of empty rentals, it may be more difficult to fill your property. Rates might have to be lowered, and you may find you must pay all the costs for the property for several months at a time while waiting to find a new renter.

Benefits of a Rental Property

Rental properties create ongoing cash flow that can last for years. They have the potential to provide a steady stream of residual income for your retirement years.

Another advantage is the rental income is received while the property (hopefully) appreciates. This means that down the road, you may be able to sell the home and receive an additional profit from the principal investment in addition to the rent that was received over the years.

Risks of a Rental Property

There are several risks involved with a rental property that need to be considered. The first is when a renter signs the lease but doesn't fulfill their agreement to pay each month. If you have selected to hire a management company, they will typically handle the eviction procedures, which vary by state. However, you may still find yourself out of several months' rent while evicting the tenant and may need to invest in repairs before the property can be rented again.

Selecting good tenants is the best way to mitigate this risk. Performing adequate due diligence is key. Running credit, verifying employment, and speaking with former landlords are all common and best practices. Speaking to the previous landlord will often provide a more accurate assessment of the kind of renter they are, but keep in mind that the current landlord may give a positive review to get a bad tenant out of his or her hair. It is also good to understand the laws of the state where the property is located. Any non-compliance with the law will extend the time the renter can remain in the home, costing you more money.

Another risk is the home will sit empty. If it takes two or three months to get the home rented, you must cover all the costs of the home from your IRA while receiving no income in return. This will often include additional costs like a home security system, maintaining the property and lawn, or leaving utilities on, which would normally be paid by the renter.

The other risk to consider is that maintenance costs could be higher than anticipated. Some investors choose to purchase annual home warranties which can spread out the maintenance costs and provide a more predictable expense structure. If the roof or HVAC system needs to be replaced, these can be very costly expenses that will reduce profitability.

Commercial Real Estate

Commercial real estate provides the opportunity to use the same skills acquired in residential real estate investing with greater profit potential. It is possible to begin with smaller commercial ventures and work your way up to large multi-million-dollar properties. In general, they are more passive investments and can provide larger profits than residential properties.

For those who understand and love the real estate market, moving to commercial real estate may be a good investment option. For those just getting started, having adequate funds, good partners, and starting small can also provide opportunities.

Profits, Taxes, and IRS Rules

If the property is invested in a tax-advantaged account, all profits are either tax-free or tax-deferred each year. If you do not need the funds to live on and refrain from taking the rental income as distributions, the rental income and appreciation will accumulate within the account without being taxed. When the property is eventually sold, all proceeds from the sale return to the account either tax-free or tax-deferred, depending on the type of account.

If the rental property is in a traditional IRA, it is important to note that the profits will be taxed as ordinary income when withdrawn from the account, which can be higher than the long-term capital gains taxation real estate would ordinarily receive. For this reason, many investors who are interested in self-directed IRA rental investments will convert a traditional IRA (or another tax-deferred account) into a Roth before investing.

All IRS rules must be followed concerning prohibited transactions and disqualified persons. This means that if you have purchased a rental home on the beach, you and everyone who is considered a disqualified person cannot use the property. You cannot hire a disqualified person to complete work on the home, even if you pay market rates. This is considered self-dealing and is disallowed by the IRS.

Non-Recourse Loans

IRAs cannot guarantee or be used as collateral for a loan. Therefore, any loan made to an IRA must be non-recourse, meaning the lender's sole source of recovery in the event of default is the property serving as collateral for the loan. If the IRA cannot repay the non-recourse loan, the non-recourse lender can take the title to the property as recourse for the default, but cannot access the IRA or other personal funds.

In essence, the only collateral of a non-recourse loan is the asset that is being financed—no other recourse is available. The lender can seize the collateral but cannot seek out the borrower for any further compensation, even if the collateral does not cover the full value of the defaulted amount. The collateral of the loan and the loan-to-value ratio become especially important in non-recourse loans. If the value of the asset declines or the default results in fees and late charges that exceed the value of the asset, the lender can only use the re-sale of the asset to recoup the amount of their loan. Home mortgages are frequently non-recourse loans.

If your IRA received a non-recourse loan to purchase an asset, there is also the possibility of triggering an Unrelated Business Income Tax (UBIT). UBITs will be discussed further in a later chapter. For now, keep in mind that although this tax may be owed on a normally tax-advantaged investment, it doesn't mean you've broken any rules. It is simply the cost of doing business when receiving non-recourse financing to your IRA.

A traditional rental investment relies on two major tools to make money: leverage and depreciation.
Leverage is the ability to put a percent down and borrow the rest. However, borrowing money to buy a property owned by your SDIRA account will incur heavy taxation. Plus, the mortgage rates are higher due to the loans having to be non-recursive.

Depreciation, which allows property owners to delay taxes, wouldn't play a role as the investment is tax-free anyway.

Rental Property Summary

Rental properties is an excellent long term investment but if done with an SDIRA, you will need to avoid getting a loan because that will expose you to the very high income tax for Unrelated Business Income. You can invest in a rental property but you will have to own the property out-right.

4.3 Raw Land

"Buy land, they're not making it anymore."

- Mark Twain, writer and humorist

Raw land is any land that is in its natural state. In our vast country, finding raw land is not difficult, but finding land that will be a good investment is an entirely different story. The good news is that land has some intrinsic value and therefore may be a wise investment. Some factors can make land a bad purchase and others can bring fast and profitable returns.

Land Selection

Land can be used for many purposes, and the function it will be used for in the future will greatly impact the value of the land. Location cannot be underestimated when it comes to the purchase of land as the location is crucial to its value. The other thing to consider when evaluating land is zoning or use. Both current and future uses, as well as the speed of appreciation for the parcel, are major factors in determining the value. For these reasons, knowing the purpose of the land, along with understanding its location, will be key factors in evaluating whether or not it may be a good investment.

Location and Use of Land

Land is typically purchased with one of the following results in mind: as a long-term holding; for use or development; or as a speculative investment.

Long-term holdings are similar to rental properties in the sense of the buy-and-hold approach. Investing in raw land is a form of real estate that, like the previous chapters discussed for rehabs, rentals, and commercial property, holds intrinsic value.

Raw land investors who purchase long-term holdings understand the variety of uses for the parcel—build and develop, rent/lease, farm, mining, and beyond. They understand they can sub-divide the land to create multiple potential sources of income from a single lot. Raw land investors using a buy-and-hold approach are also anticipating the parcel to appreciate in value during the time it is held.

The majority of raw land investments are longer-term investments and the buy-and-hold approach can be combined with the next two methods we discuss. Long-term holdings do not necessarily have to be speculative in nature.

Purchase for use or development means buying a lot of land and then either developing it directly, preparing the land to be sold to a developer, or repurposing the land to create cash flow.

All of these methods generally will require more time and resources than simply buying a piece of land and holding it until demand increases to the point that money can be made on the sale. This type of investment is more strategic. Perhaps the land is zoned for single-family homes and the buyer believes they can have the land rezoned for business or commercial use. Rezoning can open the door to development that is currently unavailable.

Another option is to purchase a parcel of land and add water, sewer, and electric utilities to make it more appealing to a developer. It is important to understand the costs associated with these types of investments as they can become cost-prohibitive if the land is not located close to current sources of utilities.

Another common use for land is purchasing a larger lot that can be prepared for development and then be subdivided. This enables the investor to sell several smaller lots with more profit potential than the single lot purchased initially. Investors also look for alternate uses of the land. If the land is currently wooded acres, an investor can purchase the land and then sell the timber. Understanding what kind of trees are on the property and what the timber is worth is important when evaluating these investments.

Raw land can also be converted to farmland. You don't need to become a farmer, though, as many small farms are leased to individuals or groups who will work the land and split the profits gained from the crop or pay a monthly lease to the landowner. Many crops can be grown on small acreage, and with the popularity of farm-to-table sustainability, it is not difficult to find restaurants willing to purchase crops, especially those that are grown organically. Organically grown crops can produce a premium price over crops on which pesticides are used. Developing a farm or other alternative use for the parcel can result in land with a higher value. This can make it easier to sell, especially if cash flow has been established.

Benefits of Investing in Land

Acquiring land is generally thought of as a long-term investment. Even if only moderate growth occurs in the area, land can often increase in value over time. There is also the chance that economic growth can dramatically increase the land's value.

If the land is located where economic growth is obvious, it will be more difficult to secure a low price for the land since most investors will also see it as a solid investment. This will increase the demand and thus the price.

Finding land that is in less obvious locations can provide the greatest potential for returns, though it may take more time and research to achieve. Thinking outside the box is important for raw land investments. This might include investing in property around a less popular lake, where the surrounding area has begun encouraging more development. Another example might be buying land in an up-and-coming community. As the demand for homes around the area increases, the land value will increase.

Risks of Investing in Land

A few factors that cause land to depreciate are environmental hazards and community decline. If land is purchased in an area where there is an economic decline or it becomes a crime-ridden area, property values will plummet along with the price of the land. If the land is in an area where an environmental hazard is located, or even on the land itself, it will significantly impact the value of the land. This may also include a nuclear plant located nearby, a major highway running too close to the property, or unsealed gas tanks underground on the property. All of these situations could result in a decline in value. Investigative homework on the lot that is for sale, and also the surrounding community, may help reduce the chances of investing in a property that will have complications down the road.

The most common risk to consider when investing in land is that it is an illiquid asset, which means it is more difficult to convert into cash. Real estate as an asset class is considered to be illiquid and raw land is the most illiquid of all real estate. Consequently, the money invested in raw land should be earmarked as a long-term investment. Monthly income should not be anticipated unless the development strategy will provide an income stream. For the most part, land is initially an expense rather than an income-producing property. While you own the land, you will have to maintain and manage it until you find a suitable buyer. Knowing what the land will be used for and carefully researching the proposed use will reduce the risk of purchasing an undesirable parcel.

You must stay on top of taxes and any maintenance costs while owning the land. Generally, taxes are the main expense of owning land, but if the taxes are not paid the county can sell the property to collect the taxes owed. Additionally, if the land is located within a community or development, there may be assessments or association dues that need to be maintained as well.

Profits, Taxes, and IRS Rules

Finding the right parcel in the best location is mostly about seeing what others do not see and anticipating growth that is not obvious. Understanding the zoning process and following city and county development could give you a tremendous advantage in the selection of raw land. As most of this information is public, getting involved in the community in which you wish to invest is perhaps the best strategy for maximizing profits on land purchases.

Land held in a Roth IRA will grow tax-free, regardless of how long the property is held. This allows you to make the most profitable decision without having to consider the tax consequences of a sale. Since land acquisition often costs money during the time the raw land is held, it is necessary to have enough cash in the account to cover expenses like taxes and assessments. While these change from year to year, they are fairly predictable expenses. If the investor wishes to develop the land, cost considerations must be evaluated to ensure there is enough in the account to develop the land and still make a profit.

Land owned in a traditional IRA will offer tax-deferred savings. The funds will be taxed as ordinary income upon withdrawal from the account. For this reason, many land investors seek to convert the deferred-tax investment accounts to a Roth IRA, providing longer-term, tax-free benefits.

Outside of an IRA, land is taxed based on how long the property is held. As a long-term investment, it is possible to reduce the taxable amount to the capital gains rate. Seeking advice from a trusted advisor is recommended when selecting which vehicle to use in raw land investments.

Raw Land Summary

Investing in raw land will require research, networking, a sound strategy, and creative thinking. If you're willing to put in the work, raw land can provide another avenue to grow your retirement savings. At Blue Crystal Funds, the company the author funded, raw land is one of the types of investments they make. They buy raw land and subdivide it or just improve it and resale it.

4.4 Syndications and Direct Business Investments

"Real estate investing, even on a very small scale, remains a tried-and-true means of building an individual's cash flow and wealth."

- Robert Kiyosaki, author

This section covers a wide range of investment options. These investments involve the use of private funds to support businesses and investment opportunities that are not widely published. This is a chance to truly personalize an investment portfolio by investing in specific properties while outsourcing all the work to an expert.

Many Investment Options

Private equity involves investing directly in private companies. Exchanging funding for company equity can be risky, but when it is successful there may be a significant amount of money to be made.

Direct business investments with a retirement account involve being a silent capital partner. As such, your role is to provide capital but not participate in the management of the business. This investment can come in the form of an equity exchange, lending money with an agreed rate of return, or a combination of the two.

Private-Equity – You provide the Equity

Many private-equity firms specialize in these types of investments. The upside is that it doesn't take a lot of money to invest because the companies are pooling resources from multiple investors. You don't need to put hundreds of thousands of dollars to buy an investment property, but you could start with much less than that. The idea behind business investments is to provide an influx of cash in exchange for an agreed return that enables the business to improve and increase in value.

Benefits of Investing in Businesses

Expertise. Business investing provides an opportunity to use somebody else's expertise in a particular business area to make money. You are using the expertise of somebody that needs capital. You just need to make sure they know what they are doing and you could be on your way to above-average investment returns.

Potential high rates of return. When an investor puts in capital, he or she can obtain better rates of return than traditional investments because it cuts out middle layers in exchange for the risk assumed. You enter the business as a capital investor and not as a lender. As a provider of capital, you can get better results than just lending money.

Research can mitigate risk. The risk of private equity funding and investing in businesses can be mitigated with solid research. Solid research, planning, and business savvy can make it easier to control value fluctuations.

Businesses, especially small businesses, can adjust their business strategies and innovate to improve profitability.

Downturns are not set in stone as long as corrections are made promptly. This benefit gives investors better control over their investment returns than many other investment opportunities.

Accredited Investors

Before investing in real estate syndications, there are specific eligibility requirements that investors must meet. To be eligible for a real estate syndication, you must either be an accredited or sophisticated investor.

To be classified as an accredited investor (as of 2022), you must have an annual income of at least $200,000, or $300,000 with a spouse, to meet the basic financial threshold for investment. Alternatively, a net worth that exceeds $1,000,000 also classifies an investor as accredited. Depending on the real estate syndication offering set forth by the U.S. Securities and Exchange Commission (SEC), certain real estate syndications may only be offered to accredited investors, such as a 506(c) offering.

However, many real estate syndications are also available to sophisticated investors. Sophisticated investors must have in-depth knowledge and experience, making them eligible to become passive investors because they can accurately evaluate the merits and demerits of a prospective investment before giving the signal to close the deal. Nevertheless, there is a limit to how many non-accredited investors a syndication fund can take. You will need to inquire with the investment firm you are trying to work with to see if they would take you.

Direct Investing Risks

Capital risk. It is possible to lose some of your investment, but because your investment is backed by real estate, it would be very unlikely to lose all your capital. After all, even the worst real estate property has some value to it.

Additional capital needs. Private equity and business investments often need more than one influx of cash. Additional funds may be needed down the road to get the company in a place where it has significantly increased in value. An investor needs to be prepared to meet these needs.

Economic risk. The success of businesses can be dependent upon market conditions. When the economy is strong, a poorly run company can still find success. When the economy contracts, it tends to weed out the weaker companies with less cash to withstand slower sales. Good management and efficient operations can help offset this to some degree. Long-term recessions and economic downturns can weaken even well-managed companies. It is not always possible to predict the economic development or decline of a specific area or unforeseen developments in the industry. This can result in a loss of money or lower returns than anticipated.

Syndications and Direct Investment Summary

Syndications and capital-only investments in businesses allow you to rip the benefits of somebody else's knowledge around some specific areas of real estate, making you more money than you would do on your own. Also, syndications allow you to participate in large projects with any amount of capital you may have as the money is pooled from many investors.

Keep in mind that to take advantage of the tax benefits of SDIRA accounts, the companies where you invest will need to be companies that are transparent from the IRS point of view. Those are LLCs and sub-chapter S corporations that transfer all tax liability to the investors. Also you must be a hands-off investor and can't participate in the management of the operations.

4.5 Notes and Mortgages

Nearly everyone is familiar with the concept of debt. We borrow constantly via credit cards, car loans, and mortgages.

As with any debt, there is a borrower and a lender. The borrower is generally the individual and the lender is generally the bank. Banks have made millions of dollars over the years as lenders. Now individuals can put themselves in the lender's seat and benefit from investment returns similar to the profits banks have experienced for years.

A variety of regulatory developments and the consolidation among banks has left fewer and larger lending institutions for individuals to turn towards. As it has become more difficult to obtain financing, some investors have turned toward the democratization of capital and realized self-directed IRA and other retirement money can be utilized as a source of financing, providing capital to those seeking funds and profit potential to the investor.

Lending Defined

As we've showcased earlier in this book, some investors have used their self-directed retirement accounts to issue loans or to purchase existing loans. They can receive the loan and interest payments tax-free or tax-deferred back into their retirement account as another option to build retirement wealth. When it comes to lending or borrowing money, there are two basic types of loans: secured loans and unsecured loans. You may also have heard the term "note," which is a document defining the terms and conditions of the loan.

Unsecured loans are also called signature loans. This would be equivalent to a credit card or a student loan. The loan is backed by the full faith and credit of the person taking out the loan. Borrowers like signature loans because they are fast and easy to manage. From a lender's perspective, these loans carry higher risk. If the borrower does not repay the loan, the lender has no real way of collecting the borrowed amount, thus increasing the risk.

Unsecured loans are heavily based on credit. While borrowers get heartburn thinking about managing credit and maintaining a high credit score, the lenders regard it as a great tool. Credit scores monitor how well we pay our bills and provide the lender with a written track record of how responsible we are. Therefore, the higher the credit score, the more responsible the borrower generally is in paying off their debt—the lower the risk, and the lower the interest rate that is offered. This helps the lender assess risk and mitigate the possibility of default with an accompanying interest rate that reflects that risk.

Credit is very important when loaning money, especially with riskier unsecured loans. While this is true for any investment, performing due diligence and doing your homework on the borrower becomes even more important for unsecured loans. Unsecured loans are generally discouraged from a risk perspective, but in certain circumstances may be appropriate.

Secured loans are also called collateralized loans. This means that the loan is backed by a form of collateral or something of value that can be seized in the event the borrower defaults on the loan.

An example of a secured loan would include a car loan. Credit is still a factor when assessing secured loans, but the collateral is as important as the credit. If the borrower chooses not to make payments on the loan or goes into default, the lender has the opportunity to get repaid for the loan by taking possession of the collateral. In the car business, this is called repossession, more commonly referred to as a repo. In the real estate business, it is called a foreclosure.

Secured loans have a lower risk of non-payment because the borrower will lose something important to him, such as the collateral of his home or car. As a result, the default rate is often lower so the interest rate is also lower to reflect the reduced risk. Investors prefer secured loans because they can receive a nice return on their investment, but also have a way to recoup their investment if the borrower fails to make payments on time.

There are two basic types of secured loans: recourse loans and non-recourse loans. As a lender, understanding the difference is increasingly important. It is also critical to understand the difference as a self-directed IRA investor since IRAs can only receive non-recourse loans.

Recourse loans give the lender more power and access to the borrower's other assets to be repaid should the borrower default on the loan. In this case, if the sale of the collateral does not fully pay off the loan, the lender can seek recourse on additional assets. Car loans are commonly recourse loans. If the insurance company does not completely pay off a wrecked car, the borrower is still often responsible for the balance of the loan.

It is also important to understand liens and lien positions when evaluating a loan. When a buyer obtains a loan for a home, the lender goes to the courthouse and files a lien on the collateral that was used to secure the loan. With a vehicle, the lien is filed with the DMV and corresponding insurance company. A lien is a legal way to announce that the lender has a claim on the property. As a lender, the lien process secures the collateral, and if the process is not completed properly, the lender will essentially have an unsecured loan and a higher risk.

Liens are rated by position. There is generally only one lien in a vehicle loan because a car is a depreciating asset, meaning it loses value over time. However, homes can often have more than one lien. Therefore, the lien position determines who gets paid first in the event of a foreclosure.

As a lender, it is critical to understand the lien position and how to protect that position. In general, liens are prioritized by the date the lien is filed at the courthouse. The two exceptions are tax liens and IRS liens. If the property taxes are not paid, the county will place a lien on the home (tax liens are another popular investment strategy covered in a previous chapter).

Property tax liens will always be in the first lien position and will take precedent over a mortgage or any other lien. For this reason, mortgage holders require taxes to be paid on time and encourage an escrow account where money is placed each month to ensure the lender pays the taxes. IRS liens for back taxes are another type that takes priority over a mortgage.

As you can see, determining lien position and researching an investment opportunity for undisclosed liens or encumbrances is an important part of the due diligence process.

Loan-to-value (LTV) ratio has a major impact on risk in secured investments. This is the value of the asset compared to the value of the loan. In real estate, the LTV ratio considers what the property can be sold for compared to the amount that is borrowed.

For example, if the home appraises for $100,000 and the loan is for $80,000, there is an 80% loan-to-value ratio, or the loan is 80% of the value of the property. The lower the loan-to-value ratio, the lower the risk the lender has of not being repaid because they will be able to sell the asset to pay the loan off in full or very nearly in full.

Benefits of Investing in Notes

Along with real estate, note investing is one of the more popular alternative investment options self-directed IRA investors utilize to grow their retirement. Some investors use their self-directed IRA to serve as the lender and issue promissory notes for agreed-upon rates of return. Others purchase existing notes (mortgages) with the hope they can provide a source of passive income for their retirement.

Like any investment, there are benefits and risks associated with this asset class that must be carefully considered.

Residual income. Acting as a lender can provide the investor with a steady monthly income and more predictable returns. You can determine how much is needed in income each month and then invest in notes, mortgages, or deeds of trust that can provide the level of income you desire. As with all loans, the terms are established upfront. You will typically know the interest rate, the amount and timing of the payments, and the duration or term of the loan. This can provide reliable and ongoing income for the investor without the work required with other residual channels, such as rental property.

Passive investment. You can gain the benefits of a real estate investment without the hassles of finding tenants, collecting rent, or making repairs. You can lend the money and be paid a rate of interest each month in a more passive role.

May not require large amounts of money. When thinking of mortgages, we often think a large amount of money is needed to get in the game. Mortgage notes make it possible to invest partially in a mortgage. This allows several investors to fund a single loan. Investments can also be made on seasoned loans with shorter terms. The advantage is creating a diversified portfolio of notes that does not rely on one individual borrower for repayment. This way, if a borrower is slow to pay, other notes can help keep the returns stable. Due to this benefit, structuring your note portfolio with short- and long-term notes may be a wise investment strategy.

Risks of Investing in Notes and Mortgages

Non-payment risk. There is the risk that the borrower or borrowers will stop making payments. To mitigate this risk, many investors choose to deal exclusively in secured notes, which offer a repayment option if the borrower defaults. However, it often requires a time-consuming process of foreclosure and may tie up your funds. Thus the collateral must be acceptable to you in case it ever gets to that point.

Early payment risk. Most loans today do not have an early payment penalty. This means that the investor may be counting on a 30-year loan with steady payments, but the loan may be paid off in five or 10 years. You may think this is a good thing because you did not lose any money in the deal, but the profit in note investing often comes from the residual income derived from the interest and principal payments, which you lose out on when the loan is paid off early. Plus, the investor would need to find a new investment at the market rate to grow their portfolio as originally planned. This can create uncertainty in the residual income and may cause an unwanted hiccup in your financial planning.

Interest rate risk. As with any long-term investment, interest rate risk is a concern. This is the risk that the loan will be locked into a low rate. If the interest rates rise, you are still paid the fixed interest rate for as long as the property owner maintains the loan. You may find yourself looking enviously at comparable investments with much higher interest rates. However, if the rates go down, the payments are locked in at a higher rate. Though, the property owner may choose to refinance the loan with another lender, thus paying the loan off early.

Decline in value. One should also consider the risk that the real estate will decline in value. If the property owner destroys the property, there is a fire or other natural disaster, or the location declines significantly in value, the real estate can decline below the amount of the note.

Requiring insurance may be a way to mitigate this risk. Many investors start by verifying the location of the property and determining the local real-estate climate and then require property insurance. A third way to mitigate this risk is to seek investments with a lower loan-to-value ratio, therefore ensuring that a decline will not significantly impact the ability to sell the home to pay off the loan, if needed.

Notes and Mortgages Summary

Notes and mortgages are usually secured by real estate and can help to reduce the risk. This allows you to invest in real estate without the legwork of finding and managing properties. It can also provide steady residual income if you're looking for ongoing payments. As loans are paid off, new investments can be made to ensure adequate cash flow.

It is common for investors to purchase seasoned loans, meaning loans that have a payment track record. This enables investors to get a feel for the borrower's payment history, thus reducing the overall risk. These investments are considered long-term because the notes may be difficult to sell on the secondary market and the borrower cannot be compelled to pay the loan off early in the event the investor needs the funds. Therefore it is best to invest in mortgage notes for the cash flow, recognizing that the principal investment may be tied up for the term of the loan.

4.6 Tax Liens

> *"Every person who invests in well-selected real estate in a growing section of a prosperous community adopts the surest and safest method of becoming independent, for real estate is the basis of wealth."*
>
> *- Theodore Roosevelt, U.S. president*

Many people refer to tax liens in a broad manner, including two categories: tax liens and tax deeds. In a strict sense, when one acquires a tax lien, one is buying a debt. Whereas with a tax deed, the property itself is acquired.

This chapter will deal with tax liens in the strict sense of the word and we'll dedicate another chapter to tax deeds.

Real estate property taxes are generally determined by the county in which the property is located and are due to the county each year. The revenue the county generates from collecting property taxes helps to fund the expenses of operating the county government. This can include fire and police services, road construction, educational expenses, parks and recreational maintenance, and many other services the county provides.

When property owners neglect to pay their property taxes, the county has difficulty meeting their financial obligations. As a result, 29 states, the District of Columbia, Puerto Rico, and the Virgin Islands issue tax liens and hold tax-lien sales. Tax-lien sales are used to fund the government while property owners are given additional time to pay back the taxes they owe.

Tax Liens and Tax-Lien Certificates

When taxes become delinquent, the county will put a lien on the property. The advantage of a tax lien is that it supersedes all other liens on the property. If there is a mortgage lien, a mechanics lien, or even an IRS lien, the tax lien will take the first lien position on the property. This means if the property is sold or foreclosed upon, the tax lien will be repaid before any other liens.

When the county decides to sell a tax lien, it will often issue a tax-lien certificate to the investor. This certificate gives the investor the right to receive the value of the tax lien in addition to any penalties and interest that is owed by the taxpayer. It does not give the investor the right to enter the property or obtain the property during the redemption period. The details of the lien will be outlined in the tax-lien certificate, such as how much is owed, the interest rate, how long the redemption period lasts, and if there are any penalties associated with the lien. If the property owner does not repay any back taxes, interest, and penalties owed before the redemption period set by the state expires, the investor has the right to foreclose on the property.

Benefits of Tax-Lien Investing

Secured collateral. Tax liens offer one of the more secure forms of collateral available in the alternative space. The tax lien is secured by the property. It obtains the first lien position, meaning that if for any reason the property owner does not pay the lien, the investor will have the first rights to the property in the event of foreclosure. In essence, the worst-case scenario is you end up with the property that you bid on (assuming you win the bid). This is why selecting a tax-lien property that you feel comfortable "getting stuck with" is so important when conducting your due diligence.

High-interest rates. Many property owners of tax-lien properties will eventually pay off the lien during the redemption period. This can provide a relatively safe investment for investors seeking higher rates of returns on their investments. Interest rates can range from 5% to 36%, depending on the state or the county where the tax lien is purchased. Additional penalties may also apply and may add to the return.

In a competitive auction, it is possible the interest rate is bid down or the price of the tax lien is bid up. Naturally, this can impact the overall return of the investment. As property owners pay their delinquent taxes, the investor will receive a check for the tax lien's face value plus interest and penalties.

Some tax-lien investors can work with the property owners to reduce the taxes that are owed or the interest being charged since the investor was able to acquire the property at a substantial discount from the county at the auction. This creates a situation where the property owner can benefit from reduced taxes owed and can remain on their property, the investor benefits from the interest payments that are made, and the county benefits because they were able to recoup a portion of the taxes that were owed so they can continue to fund their financial obligations.

Lower initial investment. When people think of real estate investing, they often think large amounts of money are needed to participate. Tax liens can be an exception to this rule. The taxes owed on a property are generally small in comparison to the property's overall value. Tax rates vary widely from state to state and county to county. Even if the taxpayer has not paid in two or three years, you might be able to invest a few thousand dollars and win a tax lien. In smaller counties with fewer services, liens can be obtained for a few hundred dollars. This enables small-dollar investors the opportunity to get involved in the market of tax liens.

Risks of Tax-Lien Investing

An important consideration in tax-lien investing is the property's value. While some tax-lien sales are now completed online, there is no substitute for physically seeing the property, especially if you are just starting out as a tax-lien investor. If you begin investing closer to home, you will know the area and be able to drive by the property before the sale and get an estimate on what the property is worth. The higher the value compared to the lien amount, the better. Try to find local investors or others familiar with the area to paint a more complete picture of the properties at the tax-lien auction.

Watch for properties that have sustained significant damage. Past events such as fires and floods will impact the value of the property and may cause the property to be worth less than the taxes due. Another area of concern is neighborhoods that are being abandoned. Consider why the neighborhood is being abandoned and why the owner no longer wants the property or is willing to refrain from paying taxes and accept foreclosure. If this is the case, it may be in an area that will be difficult to rent or sell should you end up owning the parcel.

Other concerns and risks may include the owner filing bankruptcy, tax liens that are sold incorrectly, if the lien only includes improvements to the property (and not the land), special assessments, EPA sites (with potential environmental hazards), and common property or land-locked property.

Another important note: if you purchase a tax lien, you must keep up with the property taxes and other expenses. If there is a two- or three-year redemption period and the property owner is not paying the taxes and interest, you will be required to pay each year until the redemption period has expired. This is especially important if your IRA owns the property since your IRA will need to have enough funds available to carry the property until the lien redeems or expires. You should also make sure there is a clean title to the property and that you have performed your due diligence before investing.

Ownership (or lack thereof) on Tax Liens

While getting a high rate of interest is the primary strategy for some investors, others are focused on the percentage of liens that do not catch up with their taxes, in hopes of obtaining the physical property at an extreme discount. Each county has different laws regarding tax liens. All tax liens have a redemption period during which the property owner can catch up on the back taxes, including interest and penalties to maintain the property.

Once the redemption period has expired, the tax-lien certificate holder can foreclose on the property to obtain the deed. A tax deed is issued, allowing the tax-certificate holder to obtain rights to the property. Generally, they will gain the property without any liens or encumbrances.

There is a time between when the redemption period has expired and the tax-lien certificate holder must foreclose on the property. If this timeframe passes and the investor does not foreclose on the property, the tax-lien certificate can become worthless. For this reason, only starting in a few counties is a way to learn the system before branching out to tax lien investing on a larger scale.

Profits, Taxes, and IRS Rules

The interest earnings gained from tax liens are taxed as ordinary income if not purchased within a tax-advantaged account. Ordinary income is the taxes paid at the highest tax bracket and is determined by your combined overall income.

The county will require a W-9 to be completed when you purchase a tax lien. This provides the information needed for the county to report the interest paid to the IRS. If the tax lien is purchased in a traditional IRA, the interest paid will be received tax-deferred, and if it is being purchased by a Roth IRA, then the interest will be received tax-free.

If you purchase a lien with an 18% interest payment for 36 months, you're investing in 36 months of tax-free or tax-deferred profits that can grow within the account. Even more importantly, if you purchase a tax lien within a self-directed IRA, the value of the property when the lien is sold is sheltered within the tax advantages of your account.

Tax Lien Summary

Tax-lien certificates can provide investors with higher rates of interest than CDs, money markets, bonds, and other interest-bearing accounts. The risk is low insofar as the investment is secured by real estate and property owners can often pay the tax lien off (with interest) before the redemption period expires.

The collateral helps to make tax liens a relatively safe investment. Generally, redemption periods range from a few months to a few years. This means that the investor's funds will be tied up during that time. They also run the risk of the investment being paid off quickly, resulting in a lower return on the investment as less interest is accrued during the condensed period of time. Buying a portfolio of several tax liens is one way to mitigate this risk as new tax liens will replace the ones that are paid off.

As with all investments, it is important to understand the market. Speak with county office personnel and learn about the procedures and rules within the county you are interested in purchasing tax liens. They are a good resource since each county operates its auctions differently.

4.7 Tax Deeds

"Nothing will give you better returns"

- Anonymous person at a tax sale auction

Tax deeds and tax liens, as described earlier in the book, are very similar. But a critical distinction is that with a tax deed you acquire the property, usually with a defeasible title—that is, a title that can be recovered by the former owner.

The rules regarding tax deeds vary by state so make sure to check local regulations before investing. When property owners neglect to pay their property taxes, the county will face difficulty meeting their financial obligations. As a result, counties in about 20 states will auction off the properties in public auctions and sell them to the highest bidder.

Tax Deeds

When taxes become delinquent, the county will execute a fieri facias (FIFA) on the property, which gives them the right to sell it. The county or city will then auction off the property and sell it to the highest bidder. The buyer then purchases the property free of other mortgages or liens, except for IRS or state liens.

When the county sells a property under a tax deed, the deed confers property to the buyer subject to a right of redemption by the former owner or prior lien holders. The time of the right of redemption varies from estate-to-estate and even by type of property. Once again, it is critical that local laws be checked.

The former owners or lien holders can redeem the property but have to pay a fee, interest, or penalty that varies by state. If the former property owner does not repay any back taxes, interest, and penalties owed before the redemption period set by the state expires, the investor has the right to foreclose on the right of redemption and acquire the full title to the property.

Benefits of Tax Deed Investing

Secured collateral. Tax deeds offer one of the more secure forms of collateral available in the alternative space. The tax deed is secured by the property. If the former owner does not pay to redeem the property, you now have a property for which you paid a below-market price. But to get to this point, you must conduct proper due diligence research to make sure you do not overpay at auction time.

High interest rates. Many property owners of tax-deed properties will eventually redeem the property and pay the fees. In some states, the fees owed to the tax-deed buyer can be as high as 25% of the amount paid, making them very attractive to investors.

Lower prices. Properties sold in action usually sell for less than market value. So if you end up owning the property, you would have paid a low price for it.

Risks of Tax-Deed Investing

An important consideration in tax-deed investing is the property's value. You must have a clear idea of the value of the property you are buying but you can't really do a proper inspection. You can only assess property value by visually inspecting it from the outside.

While some tax-deed sales are now completed online, there is no substitute for physically seeing the property. Watch for properties that have sustained significant damage. Past events such as fires and floods will impact the value of the property and may cause the property to be worth less than the taxes due.

Another area of concern is neighborhoods that are being abandoned. Consider why the neighborhood is being abandoned and why the owner no longer wants the property or is willing to refrain from paying taxes and accept foreclosure. If this is the case, it may be in an area that will be difficult to rent or sell should you end up owning the parcel. Other concerns and risks may include the owner filing bankruptcy and tax deeds that are sold incorrectly.

Another important note: if you purchase a tax deed, you must keep up with the property taxes and other expenses. If there is a two- or three-year redemption period and the property owner is not paying the taxes and interest, you will be required to pay each year until the redemption period has expired. This is especially important if your IRA owns the property since your IRA will need to have enough funds available to carry the property until the lien redeems or expires.

Ownership (or lack thereof) on Tax Liens

While getting a high rate of interest is the primary strategy for some investors, others may be focused on the properties that are not going to be redeemed. Most tax deeds have a redemption period during which the property owner can catch up on the back taxes, including interest and penalties, to maintain the property. Once the redemption period has expired, the tax-deed certificate holder can foreclose the right of redemption to have full ownership of the property (also known as having a "Fee Simple deed").

Taxes on tax deeds gains

The interest earnings gained and the capital gains earned from tax deeds are taxed as ordinary income if not purchased within a tax-advantaged account. Ordinary income is the taxes paid at the highest tax bracket and is determined by your combined overall income.

Tax Deed Summary

Tax-deed properties can provide investors with higher rates of interest than CDs, money markets, bonds, and other interest-bearing accounts. They can also provide properties at a lower than fair-market value. The risk is high considering you can't assess the real value of the property due to being unable to set foot on it before buying it.

The collateral helps to make tax liens a relatively safe investment. Generally, redemption periods range from a few months to a few years. This means that the investor's funds will be tied up for that period of time.   At Blue Crystal Funds, the company funded by the author, they invest in tax deeds with great success.

Appendixes

Appendix 1 - Tax Deed and Tax Lien Estates

Alabama
> Type: Lien
> Interest: 12%
> Redemption: 1 to 3 years

Alaska
> Type: Deed
> Interest: -
> Redemption: None

Arizona
> Type: Lien
> Interest: 16%
> Redemption: 3 years

Arkansas
> Type: Deed
> Interest: -
> Redemption: 1-3 years

California
> Type: Deed
> Interest: -
> Redemption: 1 year

Colorado

Type: Lien
Interest: Fed + 9%
Redemption: 3 years

Connecticut
Type: Lien
Interest: 18%
Redemption: 6 months

Delaware
Type: Deed
Interest: 15%
Redemption: 60 days

Florida
Type: Lien
Interest: 18%
Redemption: 2 years

Georgia
Type: Deed
Interest: 20% First year, then 10%
Redemption: 1 year

Hawaii
Type: Deed
Interest: 12%
Redemption: 1 year

Idaho
Type: Deed
Interest:

Redemption:

Illinois
Type: Lien
Interest: 18-48%
Redemption: 2-3 years

Indiana
Type: Lien
Interest: 10-30%
Redemption: 1 year

Iowa
Type: Lien
Interest: 24%
Redemption: 2 years

Kansas
Type: Deed
Interest: -
Redemption: 2 years

Kentucky
Type: Lien
Interest: 12%
Redemption: 1 year

Louisiana
Type: Lien
Interest: 12% +
Redemption: 3 years

Maine

Type: Deed
Interest: -
Redemption: -

Maryland
Type: Lien
Interest: 6% +
Redemption: Varies

Massachusetts
Type: Lien
Interest: 16%
Redemption: Varies

Michigan
Type: Deed
Interest: -
Redemption: -

Minnesota
Type: Deed
Interest: -
Redemption: -

Mississippi
Type: Lien
Interest: 18% +
Redemption: 2 years

Missouri
Type: Lien
Interest: 10%
Redemption: 2 years

Montana

Type: Lien
Interest: 10% +
Redemption: 3 years

Nebraska

Type: Lien
Interest: 14%
Redemption: 3 years

Nevada

Type: Deed
Interest: -
Redemption: -

New Hampshire

Type: Lien
Interest: 18%
Redemption: 2 years

New Jersey

Type: Lien
Interest: 18% +
Redemption: 2 years

New Mexico

Type: Deed
Interest: -
Redemption: -

New York

Type: Both
Interest: 12%
Redemption: 2 years

North Carolina
Type: Deed
Interest: -
Redemption: -

North Dakota
Type: Deed
Interest: -
Redemption: -

Ohio
Type: Both
Interest: 18%
Redemption: 1 year

Oklahoma
Type: Deed
Interest: -
Redemption: -

Oregon
Type: Deed
Interest: -
Redemption: -

Pennsylvania
Type: Deed
Interest: -

Redemption: -

Puerto Rico
Type: Lien
Interest: 20%
Redemption: 1 year

Rhode Island
Type: Lien
Interest: 10% +
Redemption: 1 year

South Carolina
Type: Lien
Interest: 12% +
Redemption: 1 year

South Dakota
Type: Lien
Interest: 10%
Redemption: 3 years

Tennessee
Type: Deed
Interest: 10%
Redemption: 1 year

Texas
Type: Deed
Interest: 25% +
Redemption: Varies

Utah
Type: Deed
Interest: -
Redemption: -

Vermont
Type: Deed
Interest: 12%
Redemption: 1 year

Virgin Islands
Type: Lien
Interest: 12%
Redemption: 1 year

Virginia
Type: Deed
Interest: -
Redemption: -

Washington DC
Type: Lien
Interest: 18%
Redemption: 6 months

Washington
Type: Deed
Interest: -
Redemption: -

West Virginia
Type: Lien
Interest: 12%

Redemption: 18 months

Wisconsin
Type: Deed
Interest: -
Redemption: -

Wyoming
Type: Lien
Interest: 15% +
Redemption: 4 years

Appendix 2 – Keywords in investing and real estate.

1031 - See: Tax-deferred exchange.

Abatement - The reduction, decrease, or elimination of a tax previously assessed.

Absentee Bidding - A process by which a bid may be submitted without the presence of the person submitting it, such as: by mail, by phone, by an assistant, etc.

Abstract (aka Abstract of Title) - 1. A condensed history of the chain of title to land, including (but not limited to) a statement of all liens, charges, encumbrances, and liabilities the land is subject to. May also include maps and plats. 2. In Texas, the book or volume of plat maps is sometimes known as an Abstract.

Acre - A measurement of land in any shape equivalent to 43,560 square feet (160 sq. rods). 640 acres make up a section, 36 sections make up a township.

Adjusted Basis - Value used in calculating the taxable gain on the sale of a property. The adjusted basis is the original cost of the property plus capital improvements minus accumulated depreciation and the cost of selling it.

Adjustment Period - The length of time that determines how often the interest rate can change on an adjustable rate mortgage. See also: Index, Cap, and Margin.

Ad Valorem - Taxes imposed at a rate set by law or as a percentage of value.

Amortization - Creative process of retiring debt through predetermined periodic payments.

Appraisal - Evaluation or estimation of value of property by disinterested persons of suitable qualifications.

Appreciation - Increase in the market value of real estate over its value since purchase.

APR (Annual Percentage Rate) - Calculation disclosed on the Truth-in-Lending (TIL) Act, which indicates the total cost of credit when other costs are taken into account.

ARM (Adjustable Rate Mortgage) - A mortgage in which the interest rate can change.

Assessed Value - A value set by local government appraisers under the guidelines of state statutes for the express purpose of property taxation.

Assignment Purchasing - The transfer of a lien position from a government entity to a private investor. More simply stated, property liens not sold at auction are sold over-the-counter.

AU (Automated Underwriting) - Computerized system used by lenders to determine a borrower's eligibility for loan programs.

AVM (Automated Valuation Model) - A computerized system for determining the value of a property that can take the place of an appraisal.

Back-End Debt Ratio - Total debt payments (including monthly house payment plus homeowner's insurance and property taxes) divided by total monthly income.

Balloon Payment - A typically large final payment due on a loan that covers the remaining balance. Balloon payments are required when a loan is scheduled to be paid in full before the debt can be retired through monthly payments.

Bankruptcy - Proceedings against a debtor (who has been declared legally insolvent) to distribute the debtor's property among the creditors.

Baseline - Survey line used to establish township lines on a map grid. The baseline runs east and west on the grid in order to establish north and south halves of the grid.

Basis - The starting point for calculating the gain or loss on an investment, usually the purchase price.

Bidding a Premium or Bonus Amount - The bidding for any particular lien at auction begins at the total amount of delinquent taxes, plus interest accrued, penalties, and any other costs. The successful bidder is the one who offers the largest cash amount in excess of the amount due on the tax lien.

Bidding Down on a Percentage of Ownership (aka Bidding Down the Interest in a Property) - The bidding for any particular lien at auction begins at the maximum interest rate allowed by law. Investors offer bids in a declining manner (such as first 16%, then 15%, then 14%, etc.). The successful bidder is that investor who is willing to accept the least amount of interest for their investment.

Bid in (aka Bid Off) - A phrase used to describe the process whereby liens or properties are not sold at auction but are written off to the county for disposition.

BPO (Broker Price Opinion) - An informal estimate of value used for helping the lender determine the current value of a foreclosure property.

Cap - The maximum interest rate allowed for an ARM loan.

Capital - Money used for investing purposes.

Capital Gain or Loss - The net profit on an investment property that is subject to tax. Capital gains can be long-term (taxed at a lower rate) or short-term, depending on how long the property is held by any one owner.

Capital Improvement - A renovation that increases the value or useful life of a property for a period in excess of one year.

Cartographer - A maker of maps. Usually it is a department within the assessor's office, or a freestanding county department committed to the creation and maintenance of government plat and subdivision maps.

Cash Flow - The net operating income (NOI) of a property minus its debt service. See also: NOI and DS.

Cause Number - An index number assigned by the clerk of the court to lawsuits filed in civil court actions. The first two digits of the number usually identify the calendar year in which the original motion is filed, usually followed by a dash, then a series of five or six digits that identify the individual case.

Caveat Emptor - Latin term for: "Let the buyer beware."

Certificate of Purchase - See: Tax Lien Certificate.

Closing - A ritual that involves all the parties to a real estate sale who must meet and sign documents, disburse funds, and transfer ownership of the real estate.

Closing Costs - Costs incurred by a purchaser of real estate, or paid on their behalf, to complete the closing of the transaction. Listed on Good Faith Estimate (GFE) and the HUD-1.

CLTV (Combined Loan-To-Value) - The total percentage of loan-to-value with all mortgages included.

Commercial Property - Property used for business as opposed to living quarters. However, the term also covers residential real estate having five units or more.

Comparable (aka Comps) - Properties used as comparisons to determine the value of a similar property. When appraising the value of a property by comparing the price of similar, recently sold properties, important things to remember are the degree of similarity and the circumstances of sale.

Compound Interest - Interest calculated against the sum of the principal amount plus interest that has previously accrued.

Condemnation - The legal process by which the right of eminent domain is exercised. Part of this process includes determining just compensation.

Conforming Loan - A loan that adheres to all Fannie Mae and Freddie Mac requirements. See also: Sub-Prime Loan.

Contiguous Parcel - A neighboring or adjoining parcel of land, which may be in actual close contact, touching at a point or along a boundary of another property.

Contract for Deed - See: Land Contract.

Conventional Loan - A loan that doesn't require underwriting or insuring by the government (such as FHA or VA underwriting).

Conveyance - The transfer of title to land from one person or persons to another by written instrument (such as a deed).

Cost Approach - An appraisal method that starts with what it would cost to build the same structure today, depreciate it, and then add in the value of the land.

CC&Rs (Covenants, Conditions, and Restrictions) - Guidelines set forth in a subdivision plan by a developer of the land.

County Constant - The percentage of fair market value that local assessors appraise property at for taxation purposes. This percentage is not mandated by statute. It is simply a rule of thumb used in order to simplify the administration of the taxation process.

County Index Map - 1. The general map of the county with a super-imposed index relating to the parcel identification number. 2. A county map identifying the range and township designations of that county.

Cross-Collateralization - Using two or more properties as security for the repayment of a loan.

Debt Ratio - A formula that lenders often use to determine a borrower's ability to afford monthly payments on a loan. See also: Back-End Debt Ratio and Front-End Debt Ratio.

Deed - A written instrument transferring the title of real property from one entity to another. Types of deeds:

- Bargain and Sale Deed: Used in the conveyance of land title when the purchase is made for valuable consideration (not cash).
- Contract for Sale Deed: An agreement by a seller to deliver conveyance of a title upon completion of certain conditions (payments). Often used in place of a Warranty Deed when a purchase is subject to a particular claim.

- Quitclaim Deed: Transfers any title, interest, or claim a grantor may have in a property.
- Sheriff's Deed (Constable's Deed): Usually issued at the order of a court judgment by a county law enforcement officer.
- Special Warranty Deed: Used to convey the title of land in unique situations, such as multiple sellers with varying percentages of ownership to multiple buyers with varying percentages of ownership. It is limited to certain persons and/or claims.
- Tax Deed (Auditor's Deed): Transfers the title of land taken for delinquent taxes to a purchaser at a public sale.
- Trust Deed: See: Deed of Trust.
- Warranty Deed: A deed used in many states to convey fee title to real property. Prior to the common use of title insurance, a warranty deed expressed a guarantee that the title was free from defects.

Deed of Trust - An instrument now used in most states in place of a mortgage. The legal title to real property is transferred to a trustee in favor of the lender (aka beneficiary) until the borrower satisfies the terms of the contract.

Depreciation - The decline in value of a property over time, usually due to wear and tear.

Discount Rate – The rate that is used by banks and financial institutions when lending money among themselves. Sometimes used as an index for ARM loan adjustments.

Due Diligence - To take on the responsibility of performing one's own research to determine quality and/or value of a particular investment.

Due on Sale Clause - Wording in most mortgages that requires the borrower to pay the balance in full in the event that the property changes hands.

EMD (Earnest Money Deposit) - Funds put up by a prospective purchaser as a commitment to follow through on the purchase of a property.

Easement - 1. The right to use the property of another for a specific purpose, such as: for the benefit of a contiguous landowner so that he can get from parcel A to parcel B. 2. *Gross easement*: as in, a right-of-way for utility lines. Refers to the actual land used.

Egress - 1. The path by which a person exits land. 2. The act or right of going or leaving. Often used with the term *ingress* in the combination *ingress and egress* (i.e., entering and leaving), which simply means the right to come and go across the land of another.

Eminent Domain - The power to take private property for public use by federal, state, or local governments. This power is granted by the Fifth Amendment of the US Constitution. The taking of property by this device requires just compensation.

Encumbrance - A claim, lien, charge, or liability attached and/or binding to real property.

Equity - The amount of money remaining if you sold the property today and paid off any loans taken out against the property.

Escheat - A reversion of ownership of property (real or personal) to the state when there is a lack of any individual to inherit it.

Estoppel Certificate - Legal document that tenants use to acknowledge agreements or changes in the lease or the status of rent payments.

Fair Market Value - The appraised value of a property as compared with other property values on the market.

Fee Simple - 1. Typically, the words *fee simple* standing alone create an absolute estate, or one without limitations and/or conditions. Those words followed by a condition or limitation are subject to those situations. 2. A synonym for ownership.

FHA (Federal Housing Administration) - The division of the Department of Housing and Urban Development that insures home mortgage loans.

FICO (Fair Isaac & Company) Score - A credit scoring system commonly used by lenders to determine the risk a borrower represents related to repayment.

FIFA (Fieri Facias) - A term used exclusively in Georgia referring to a tax lien document or writ that authorizes the sheriff to obtain satisfaction of unpaid taxes by levying on and selling the delinquent taxpayer's property.

Final Disposition Sale - A term exclusive to Florida. After the expiration of the redemption period, tax liens in Florida are brought to a secondary sale to afford additional investors the opportunity to bid for the deed. The opening bid equals the redemption cost of the tax lien certificate. Should there be no additional bids, the lien holder is awarded the deed in exchange for the Certificate of Purchase.

Financing - The way in which an investor acquires the capital with which to purchase a property.

Fixed-Rate Loan - A loan for which the interest rate remains unchanged over the life of the loan. See also: ARM.

Foreclosure - 1. To destroy an equity of redemption. A termination of rights to real property. 2. To deprive an interested party of his rights to real estate.

Forfeiture Clause - Legal wording commonly used in a land contract or lease option agreement that entitles the seller to repossess the property in the event that the buyer fails to comply with the terms of the agreement.

Front-End Debt Ratio - House payment alone (including property taxes and insurance) divided by total monthly income. According to the FHA, your front-end debt ratio should not exceed 31%. See also: Debt Ratio and Back-End Debt Ratio.

GFE (Good Faith Estimate) - A list of estimated costs involved in a loan transaction that the lender provides to the borrower prior to, or within three days of, an application.

Goal - A purpose or objective that an individual is willing to work toward.

Grantee - One to whom a grant is made (generally, the buyer).

Grantor - One who grants property to another (generally, the seller).

Hard Money - A typically short-term, high-interest loan that investors often use to acquire some quick cash so that they can move forward on an investment opportunity.

HELOC (Home Equity Line Of Credit) - Credit line secured by a piece of real property. With an HELOC, you pay interest on only the amount of money you actually draw against the credit line.

Homestead Exemption - A reduction in the taxable value of a property as authorized by law. It can have different definitions in different states.

HUD (Department of Housing and Urban Development) - The branch of the federal government that oversees FHA.

HUD-1 - Settlement statement used at closing to disclose all costs and credits for borrowers and sellers involved in a real estate transaction.

Hybrid Loan - A combination of an ARM and a fixed-rate loan. For example, with a 3/1 hybrid, the interest rate would remain fixed for three years and then become an adjustable-rate loan in which the rate could be adjusted every year. See also: ARM and Fixed-Rate Loan.

Improvement - Buildings or other structures that become part of the land.

In Arrears - Delinquent.

Income Approach - A real estate appraisal method that focuses more on the revenue-generating potential of rental property than on the property's value.

Incorporate - The process of forming a local political body, such as a city or town, to create a municipal system.

Index - An indicator used to calculate rates on some mortgage loan products, notably ARM loans. See also: Adjustment Period, Cap, and Margin.

Index Map - A map of a taxing jurisdiction containing references to a tax identification numbering system.

Ingress - 1. Access or entrance. 2. The act or right of entering. Often used with the term *egress* in the combination *ingress and egress* (i.e., entering and leaving), which simply means the right to come and go across the land of another.

Interest - A percentage of the amount of money paid for its use over a specific time frame. Usually expressed as an annual percentage of the amount of the loan.

IRA - Individual Retirement Account.

Judgment - The verdict of a court on a matter presented to it.

Junior Lien - A mortgage or other encumbrance with a secondary interest.

Land Contract - A legal instrument that enables a seller to finance the purchase of his property. The seller functions as the lender, and the contract takes the place of a mortgage or deed of trust.

Lease - A contractual agreement between the owner and the tenant, which allows the tenant to use and occupy a property for a specific period of time.

Leasee - One who contracts to hold occupancy rights in the real property of another.

Lease Option Agreement - A legal instrument that enables a buyer to rent a property for a certain amount of time, at the end of which she has the option to purchase it for the pre-agreed-upon price.

Legal Description - The means by which a property is identified through exact boundaries. The surveyor will use the recorded plats, metes and bounds, or the government survey to describe real property.

Leverage - The use of borrowed money to increase purchasing power.

Lien - 1. A claim, encumbrance, or change on a property for payment of some debt. 2. Security for a debt. 3. The right to retain property for payment of a debt; in our case, tax debt.

Lien Certificate - See: Tax Lien Certificate.

Lis Pendens - 1. Latin term for *a suit pending*, which refers to a written notice that a lawsuit has been filed which concerns real property. 2. A common law doctrine filed in court as notice of jurisdiction, power, or control, a court will require over property in litigation, pending action until final judgment.

LLC (Limited Liability Company) - A legal structure that protects the owner's personal assets from any loss that the business incurs.

Loan Officer - Someone who works for a lending institution or mortgage broker to assist borrowers in selecting and applying for loans. See also: Mortgage Broker.

Long-Term Capital Gain - The realized profit on an investment property held more than 12 months.

LTV (Loan-To-Value) - A ratio expressing the loan amount divided by the property's current market value. For example, the LTV on an $80,000 loan to purchase a $100,000 property would be 80%. Lenders use LTV as one way to measure risk—the lower the LTV, the less the risk.

Management Expenses (ME) - Whatever you pay yourself or others to care for a property.

Margin - An amount added to an index to calculate an adjustment for an ARM loan. The margin remains constant over the life of the loan. See also: Adjustment Period, Index, and Cap.

Maturity - The date on which the principal amount of a note, draft, bond, lien, or other debt instrument becomes due and payable.

Meridian - Survey line used to establish range lines on a map grid. The meridian runs north and south on the grid in order to establish east and west halves of the grid.

Mill - The rate of tax imposed upon taxable value. One mill equals $1 of tax for every $1,000 of taxable value.

Minimum Bid - The opening price a property will be offered for at auction. See also: Opening Bid.

Mortgage - A loan secured by real estate. States which are not trust states use a mortgage as the legal instrument to secure a lien against the property.

Mortgage Broker - A licensed professional who assists borrowers in shopping for loans made available through multiple lenders.

MUD (Municipal Utilities District) - A type of taxing jurisdiction.

Net Worth - The value of everything you own minus everything you owe.

NOI (Net Operating Income) - The amount of money left over after all expenses are deducted from a property's gross income.

Non-Conforming Loan - See: Sub-Prime Loan.

Note - Legal instrument that describes the terms of the mortgage loan.

Opening Bid - 1. The beginning bid of an item at auction. Generally, the amount of all taxes, interest, penalties, and fees. 2. The first bid. See also: Minimum Bid.

Operating Expenses - Costs for maintaining a property, such as taxes, insurance, maintenance, and upkeep.

Over-the-Counter List - 1. A list of liens/properties available for sale after an auction has taken place. These liens/properties can be purchased with no competitive bidding and as an arms-length transaction. They are sold on a first-come, first-served basis.

Parcel - 1. A contiguous area of land described in a single description by a deed or other instrument. 2. A number of lots on a plat or plan, separately owned and capable of being separately conveyed.

Pass-Through Expenses - Costs that a landlord incurs and then charges the tenant to (pay in full or a portion of) in addition to paying rent.

Penalty - A sum of money attached to a debt as a punishment for nonpayment.

Per Annum - By the year (annually; yearly).

Personal Property - 1. In a general sense, everything subject to ownership that is not considered to be real property. 2. Movable assets. For taxation purposes, some examples would be: contractor's tools, farm machinery, office furniture, and so on.

PIN or PID - Parcel Identification Number (aka Parcel Number), (aka Property Number), (aka Account Number), (aka Abstract Number), (aka Folio Number), etc.

PITI (Principal Interest Taxes Insurance) - Term used to describe a payment that covers the principal and interest due on a loan along with taxes and insurance to be placed in escrow.

Plat Map (aka Subdivision Map) - A map outlining individual lots within a block or tract of land.

PMI (Private Mortgage Insurance) - Insurance required on high LTV conventional loans.

Points - Interest paid on a loan upfront rather than monthly. One point is 1% of the total loan amount.

Pre-Approval - A lender's agreement to finance the purchase of an investment property up to a certain amount, assuming the property meets certain conditions. See also: Prequalification.

Premium - The difference between the purchase price and the opening/minimum bid of a property at auction.

Premium Bidding - An opening bid that equals the sum of taxes, interest, and penalties due. Bidding continues in set dollar amount increments, increasing with each new bid.

Prepaids - Costs of a transaction listed on the GFE or HUD-1, which are paid in advance for the benefit of the borrower.

Prepayment Penalty - A clause in some mortgage agreements that requires the borrower to pay additional money if they pay back the loan early.

Prequalification - A lender's assurance that a borrower probably would qualify for a particular loan. See also: Pre-approval.

Pro Forma - A statement projecting the future performance of an income-producing property.

Promissory Note - A legal document borrowers sign as their personal agreement to pay back a loan according to the terms specified in the note.

Property ID Number - A county treasurer's way of identifying a particular property. See: PIN (aka Parcel Identification Number).

Property Profile - A report formulated by title companies identifying basic statistics of a particular property. Some companies may charge a small fee for this report, but quite often they are free.

QRP (Qualified Retirement Plan) - One in which you can control the investment decisions, including real estate tax lien investments (e.g., Self-Directed IRA).

Quiet Title Action - 1. A proceeding to establish the plaintiff's title to land by bringing into court an adverse claimant and thereby compelling him either to establish his claim or be forever after stopped from asserting it. 2. An action filed in civil court to test and/or perfect a title to real property. 3. A notice to the world of a pending claim to real property. 4. To request of the court an order to quash any and all subsequent claims.

Range - Columns of a mapping grid formed by range lines in six-mile increments. Identified as east or west of the meridian.

Real Property - 1. Land and what is generally affixed, erected, or growing upon it. 2. That which is construed as immovable, except crops. Generally, a synonym for real estate.

Recourse Clause - Legal language in a loan contract that stipulates what a lender can do to collect from a borrower who is in default on a loan.

Redemption - Refers to the procedure by which the legal property owner (the title holder) or a vested interested party (such as a tax lien investor) pays the tax collector the amount required to cancel or invalidate the tax lien on the real property.

Register of Deeds (aka County Recorder) - A government office where written instruments are recorded for public notice.

REO (Real Estate Owned) - Property owned by a bank. Sometimes you can get the bank to finance the purchase of these properties.

Reserves - Amount of liquid assets that a borrower has left after paying all costs of the transaction.

RESPA (Real Estate Settlement and Procedures Act) - Federal law that requires lenders to disclose settlement costs (GFE and HUD-1) as well as the procedures for consumer disclosure.

Review of Assessment - All real property is evaluated by local government appraisers with the express purpose of determining an assessed value in order to calculate property taxes. Property owners are afforded by law a method of disputing these values that are set for taxation purposes. This phrase describes that process of disputation.

Sealed Bid - A bid made for liens or properties at auction, which are mailed to the administrator of that sale. All bids are open at a set time, date, and place, with the highest bidder being awarded the lien or property.

Section - A division of land on a map grid 1 square mile (640 acres) in size. Each township is divided by straight lines and is comprised of 36 sections of land. Sections are then divided into halves and quarters in order to legally describe tracts or parcels of land.

Self-Directed IRA - The Individual Retirement Account (IRA) allows annual payments into a tax deferred account. Self-directed accounts allow individual investors to determine how these funds will be invested, as opposed to a trustee or administrator making those decisions.

Seller Financing - A process by which the seller of a property agrees to loan the buyer the money to purchase it. See also: Land Contract and Lease-Option Agreement.

Short-Term Capital Gain - The realized profit on an investment property held for fewer than 12 months.

Simple Interest - Interest computed against principal only.

Struck - Refers to the action taken by a taxing jurisdiction when transferring the title to a real property from a property owner to the taxing jurisdiction after a tax sale has taken place and no bids were tendered.

Subdivide - To divide a lot, tract, or parcel of land into three or more smaller lots, tracts, or parcels of land for sale or development.

Subdivision - A plat of land that has been subdivided.

Subordinate - Subject to, or junior to; occupying a lower position; inferior in order.

Sub-Prime Loan - A loan that does not adhere to Fannie Mae or Freddie Mac requirements and, as a result, typically charges more in interest and upfront costs.

Substituted Service - 1. Service of notice of pending action as authorized by statute. 2. To use a publication of notice by newspaper instead of personal service or mail.

Sub-Taxing - 1. To attach a subsequent year's tax delinquency to a pre-existing lien. 2. To endorse a properly executed Tax Lien Certificate with subsequent tax years, prior to the expiration of redemption.

Tax-Deferred Exchange - A provision of the tax code that allows investors to exchange similar kinds of properties instead of selling those properties and exposing the profits to capital gains taxes. Often referred to as a 1031 in reference to this section of the tax code.

Tax Extension - 1. The process by which the tax collector calculates the tax roll for his/her county. 2. The medium by which the actual tax roll is transferred to printing of the tax bills.

Tax Lien Certificate - The document issued by a public officer to the successful bidder at a tax lien sale. The prima facie (legally sufficient) evidence of a lien position.

TIL or TILA (Truth In Lending Act) - Federal law that requires lenders to follow certain guidelines for disclosing loan terms, including the APR. Not used on commercial properties.

Time Value of Money - The concept that a dollar today is worth more than a dollar in the future, because the dollar received today can earn interest up until the time the future dollar is received.

Title – Contains a legal description of a real estate property and lists the owner of such.

Title Insurance - The insurance policy issued by a title company insuring the accuracy of its search against claims of title defects and against loss and damage resulting from such defects.

Title Search - An examination of the public record to determine the current and prior owners of a property as well as to document liens, encumbrances, claims, and defects relating to real property.

Township - In some estates, rows of a mapping grid defining six-mile increments of land by township lines. Identified as north and/or south of the baseline.

Valuation - The estimating of property value for taxation purposes. An appraisal of real property.

Zoning Codes - A designation of letters and numbers used to divide a city or town into districts to regulate the use and/or structural and architectural design of land and buildings.

About the Author

Edward Tamayo, after a few years of very successfully investing his own self-directed IRA account in real estate, went on to fund <u>Blue Crystal Funds Corporation</u> where he keeps doing the same kind of work but this time also directing money trusted to his fund.

In Blue Crystal Funds, Mr. Tamayo invests in land and residential real estate via tax deeds and does this mostly in the state of Georgia, where he lives.

Mr. Tamayo's first degree was in engineering and at the beginning of his career worked for his father in his civil consulting firm. He then earned a master's in Computer Science at the University of Tennessee, Knoxville and went on to work for many years in Information Technology where he participated in major projects for many Fortune 500 companies.

www.ingramcontent.com/pod-product-compliance
Lightning Source LLC
Chambersburg PA
CBHW060939050726
47592CB00003B/1017